1978

1978

PEOPLES OF THE EARTH

volume three

Europe

(including U.S.S.R. west of the Urals)

THE DANBURY PRESS

(Previous page) Stone walls
have divided and subdivided
Connemara's holdings, forcing
many a poor Irish farmer's
son to cross the ocean to
America.

The publishers gratefully acknowledge help from
the following organizations:
Royal Anthropological Institute, London
Musee de l'Homme, Paris
International African Institute, London
British Museum, London
Royal Geographical Society, London
Scott Polar Research Institute, Cambridge
Royal Asiatic Society, London
Royal Central Asian Society, London
Pitt-Rivers Museum, Oxford
Horniman Museum, London
Institute of Latin American Studies, London

Publisher
ROBERT B. CLARKE
Marketing Director
ROBERT G. BARTNER
Creative Director
GILBERT EVANS

© 1972

Tom Stacey and Europa Verlag

Library of Congress Catalog Card No. 72 85614

Printed in Italy by
Arnoldo Mondadori Editore, Verona

PHOTOGRAPHIC CREDITS

Cover – **Ted Spiegel** (The John Hillelson Agency), **Eve Arnold** (Magnum from the John Hillelson Agency), **Ray Green** (Susan Griggs), **William Albert Allard** (Louis Mercier), **Elliott Erwitt** (Magnum from the John Hillelson Agency), **Marc Ribaud** (Magnum from the John Hillelson Agency), **Constantine Manos** (Magnum from the John Hillelson Agency), 2, 3 – **Alexander Low**. 9 – **Alain Nogues** (Gamma from the John Hillelson Agency). 10, 11 – **Burt Glinn** (Magnum from the John Hillelson Agency). 12, 13 – **Burt Glinn** (Magnum from the John Hillelson Agency) exc. top rt. **Marc Ribaud** (Magnum from the John Hillelson Agency). 15 – **Bruno Barbey** (Magnum from the John Hillelson Agency), **Constantine Manos** (Magnum from the John Hillelson Agency). 16, 17 – **Eve Arnold** (Magnum from the John Hillelson Agency), **Harrison Forman** (F.P.G.), **John Massey-Stewart** (Picturepoint), **Elliott Erwitt** (Magnum from the John Hillelson Agency). 18, 19 – **Burt Glinn** (Magnum from the John Hillelson Agency). 20 – **Burt Glinn** (Magnum from the John Hillelson Agency), **Alpha**. 22, 23 – **Burt Glinn** (Magnum from the John Hillelson Agency). 24 through 29 – **Eve Arnold** (Magnum from the John Hillelson Agency) exc 27 top lt. **John Topham** (Camera Press). 30 through 33 – **Ted Spiegel** (The John Hillelson Agency). 34 through 43 – **Constantine Manos** (Magnum from the John Hillelson Agency). 44, 45 – **Ken Heyman**. 46, 47 – **E. Rominger** (Camera Press), **Patrick Ward** (Sunday Times). 48, 49 – **Ken Heyman** exc. bot. rt. **E. Rominger** (Camera Press). 50 – **H. W. Silvester** (Rapho Paris). 51 – **Sabine Weiss** (Rapho New York). 52, 53 – **E. Rominger** (Camera Press), **Ken Heyman**. 55 through 59 – **Adam Woolfitt** (Susan Griggs). 60 through 69 – **Burt Glinn** (Magnum from the John Hillelson Agency). 71 – **Alain Perceval** (Photo Aerienne). 72 – **Francisco Hidalgo** (Woodfin Camp Associates), **Bryn Campbell** (Camera Press). 73 – **J. Pavlovsky** (Rapho New York), **A. D'Andrade** (Magnum from the John Hillelson Agency). 74, 75 – **Dennis Stock** (Magnum from the John Hillelson Agency), **Adam Woolfitt** (Susan Griggs), **Elliott Erwitt** (Magnum from the John Hillelson Agency). 76 – **Martine Franck** (Viva from the John Hillelson Agency). 77 – **Nicolas Tikhomiroff** (The John Hillelson Agency), **Henri Cartier Bresson** (Magnum from the John Hillelson Agency). 78 – **John Launois** (Black Star New York). 79 – **John Bulmer**. 80 – **C. Raimond-Dityvon** (Viva from the John Hillelson Agency). 81 – **Bruno Barbey** (Magnum from the John Hillelson Agency). 82 – **J. Pavlovsky** (Rapho New York), **John Launois** (Camera Press). 83 – **Adam Woolfitt** (Susan Griggs). 84 – **C. Raimond-Dityvon** (Viva from the John Hillelson Agency). 85 – **Henri Cartier Bresson** (Magnum from the John Hillelson Agency). 86 – **Bruce Davidson** (Magnum from the John Hillelson Agency). 87 – **J. Pavlovsky** (Rapho New York). 88 through 97 – **William Albert Allard** (Louis Mercier). 98, 99 – **Bryn Campbell** (Transworld Features). 100 – **Marc Ribaud** (Magnum from the John Hillelson Agency), **C. Raimond-Dityvon** (Viva from the John Hillelson Agency). 101 – **Pascal Hinous** (Réalités). 102 – **Bruno Barbey** (Magnum from the John Hillelson Agency). 103 – **Bryn Campbell** (Transworld Features), **Henri Cartier Bresson** (Magnum from the John Hillelson Agency), **Elliott Erwitt** (Magnum from the John Hillelson Agency). 104, 105 – **Ray Green** (Susan Griggs). 106 – **John Bulmer**. 107 – **Ray Green** (Susan Griggs). 108 – **John Bulmer**. 109 – **Ray Green** (Susan Griggs). 110, 111 – **John Bulmer** exc. bot. rt. **Ray Green** (Susan Griggs). 112, 113 – **Ray Green** (Susan Griggs). 114 through 117 – **Ruan O'Lochlain** exc. 115 top lt. **Alexander Low**. 118, 119 – **Eric Lessing** (Magnum from the John Hillelson Agency). 120 – **Elliott Erwitt** (Magnum from the John Hillelson Agency) exc. bot. lt. **Marilyn Silverstone** (Magnum from the John Hillelson Agency). 122, 123 – **Eric Lessing** (Magnum from the John Hillelson Agency). 124, 125 – **Ian Berry** (Magnum from the John Hillelson Agency). 126 – Sunday Times, Sport and General. 127 – Spectrum Colour Library. 128 – Photographers International, **Robin Adshead** (The John Hillelson Agency). 129 – **Sean Hignett** (Daily Telegraph), **Pat Langen** (Irish Times). 131 – **Franco Gremignani** (Black Star New York). 132, 133 – **Dmitri Kasterine** (Camera Press).

Contents

Editorial Director **Tom Stacey**

Picture Director **Alexander Low**
Executive Editors **Robert Targett**
Katherine Ivens
Art Director **Tom Deas**
Assistant Editor **Elisabeth Meakin**
Project Co-ordinator **Anne Harrison**

Research **Cheryl Moyer**
Charlotte Bruton
Elly Beintema
Philippa Galloway
Claire Waterson
Editorial Assistants **Richard Carlisle**
Rosamund Ellis
Rosemary Hartill
Xan Smiley
Design Assistants **Susan Forster**
Richard Kelly
Cartography **Ron Hayward**
Illustrations **Ron McTrusty**

Production **Roger Multon**

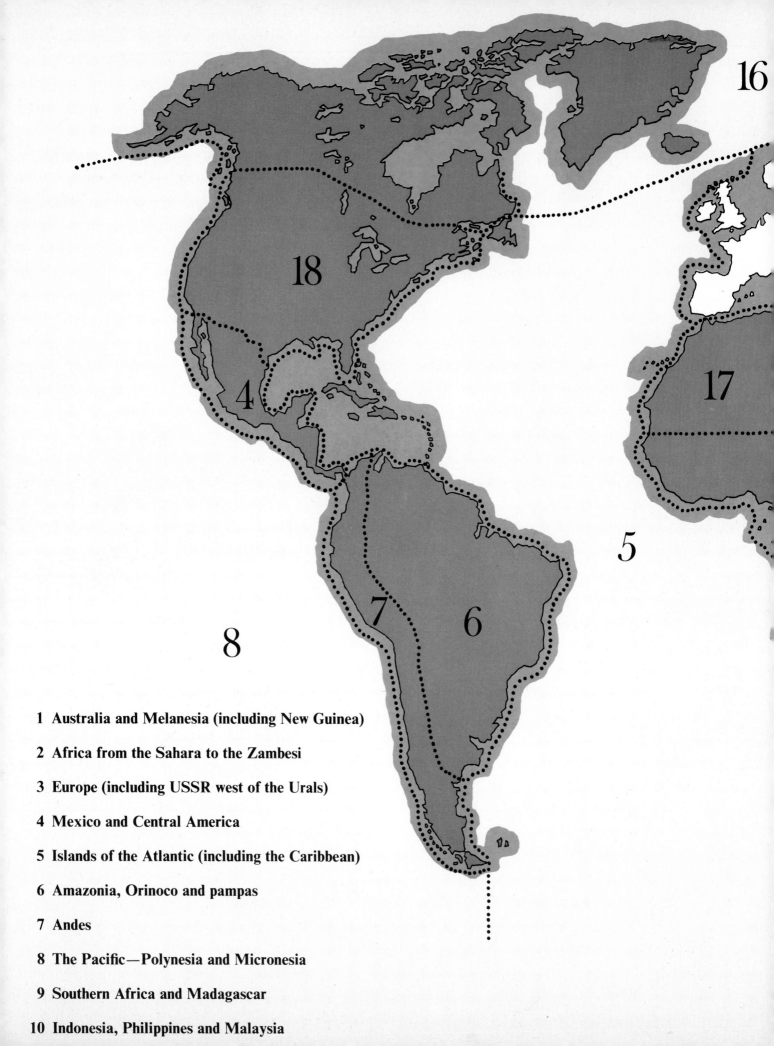

16

18

7

4

5

17

6

7

8

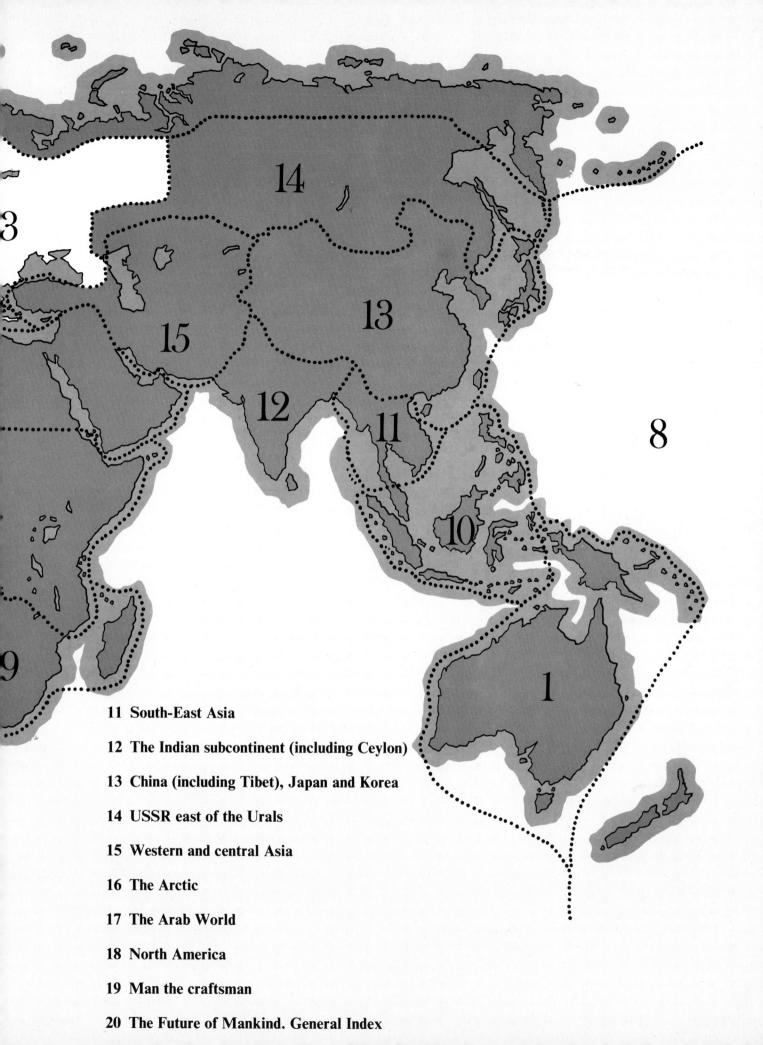

What is a nation?

The concept of nationhood is the idea that a community which does not include the whole of mankind has a paramount claim on the allegiance and devotion of the participants in this community. This claim is paramount, but of course it is not absolute. No human being is able to dedicate himself exclusively to any single loyalty. The most fanatical nationalist will have some modicum of fellow-feeling for all his fellow human beings, including the majority of them who, for him, are foreigners; and, among his fellow-nationals, he will feel a closer bond with his relatives and his friends than with strangers.

The antithesis of the concept of nationhood is the concept of ecumenicalism. Adherents of the missionary religions – Buddhism, Christianity, Islam – and now Communism too – have felt that their duty to their religion is paramount over their duty to their nation, tribe, or family, and their objective has been to propagate their religion until it becomes eventually the universal religion of all mankind. Ecumenicalism can take a secular as well as religious form. The citizens of the Chinese Empire and of the Roman Empire felt that their empire was a world state which ought to embrace all mankind and which did in fact embrace all but an unimportant outer fringe of barbarians.

The conflict between ecumenical allegiance and sectional allegiance is as old as our earliest surviving historical records. In the past, the allegiance to world-religions and to world-states has been in competition with our allegiance to tribes, to city-states, and to other sectional communities. The concept of nationhood is a new variety of sectional allegiance. This particular sectional concept arose in western Europe less than 500 years ago, and, since then, it has spread round the globe concurrently with the spread of western economic, military, and political ascendancy. These material forms of western ascendancy are now proving to be ephemeral, but at least one ideological form of western ascendancy, the ideology of nationalism, is proving more durable. Among the non-western majority of mankind, nationalism – a western ideological infection – is outlasting the west's material domination.

Today, nationalism is about 90 per cent of the religion of about 90 per cent of the human race. Present-day human beings still pay lip-service to ecumenical religions and ideologies; but, whenever the demands of ecumenicalism and nationalism conflict, nationalism invariably wins. The outbreak of World War I showed that the industrial workers in western countries were nationalists first and foremost. Their allegiance to the Second International was not strong enough to move them to disobey their national mobilization orders. The Chinese felt for 2000 years that the Chinese Empire was a world-wide community, but the impact on China of nationally-organized western powers and of a westernized Japan has turned even the Chinese into nationalists in self-defense.

In embracing Communism, the Chinese were attempting to revert to their traditional ecumenicalism in a new form. The first generation of Communists had boasted that, in the modern world, Communism was the one ideology that had a stronger hold over human hearts than nationalism. The Communists claimed that the Communist fraternity was a monolithic community that could, and did, transcend all differences of nationality, language, and race. This claim has been invalidated by events. Today, Communist China, Russia, and North Vietnam are acting just like non-Communist France, Britain, and the United States. They are each giving their respective national interests priority over their nominal common allegiance to Communism – the youngest and supposedly the most dynamic of the missionary religions whose goal is the unification of mankind.

Evidently the concept of nationhood is at present an immensely potent force – and this all round the globe, and not only in its west European birthplace. How did this modern form of sectional feeling arise originally in western Europe, and why has it been so contagious?

In western Europe till about 500 years ago, the sense of nationhood was still weak or was even non-existent. The paramount allegiance of medieval west Europeans was to the Christian religion and to the Church in which this religion was embodied. They were also conscious of local loyalties to village communities and of the personal ties between feudal lords and their vassals – not to speak of ties of kinship, which are strong at all times and places. These non-national allegiances counted for more in medieval Europe than the consciousness of being Frenchmen, Englishmen, Spaniards, or whatnot. Medieval, like modern, Europeans spoke a babel of local languages, and they were already making poetry in these languages. But for educated people, the Latin language, which was their common heritage, counted for much more, and medieval Western students, whatever their native tongue might be, felt at home in any university in western Christendom because, in all medieval western universities, Latin was the language of instruction and was also a lingua franca for personal intercourse.

How, then, did the concept of nationhood arise? It arose partly within the framework of some already established state, and partly in revolt against a state framework that was irksome. English nationhood is a product of the pre-existing Kingdom of England: British nationhood is a product of the Union of the Kingdoms of England and Scotland as recently as 1707. Present-day Scottish and Welsh and, above all, Irish nationalism is a reaction against incorporation in the United Kingdom.

The Kingdom of England, which has been the framework of English nationhood, was originally put together by the kings of Wessex (one of the local barbarian successor states of the Roman Empire in Britain). This

Arnold Toynbee

Wessex-made kingdom of England was then taken over by non-English conquerors, the Normans. In Norman England, the English-speaking population were the subjects of foreign sovereigns. It took time for the English to become masters in this foreign house, and to feel that the house was their own. The creation of English nationhood within an ex-foreign framework seems paradoxical; yet, in post-colonial Africa today, new nationhoods are in process of being created within the framework of frontiers that were imposed on the Africans by European conquerors within living memory.

In late medieval Britain and in present-day Africa, nationhood has been created by a common subjection to a government, not by a common language. In the oldest of the modern west European nations, there has, it is true, been some predominant language, but these nations have not been linguistically homogeneous. The French nation includes some non-French-speaking minorities, and the German-speaking minority of Frenchmen in Alsace and in northern Lorraine demonstrated their French national feeling when in 1871 they were forcibly annexed to the Second German Reich. Conversely, French-speaking Belgians, Swiss, and Canadians do not feel themselves to be Frenchmen. The nationhood of the Swiss is as solid as any nationhood anywhere; yet in Switzerland four languages are spoken, and even the language of the 10,000 Romansch-speaking Swiss enjoys official status.

The notion that all the speakers of a particular language ought to be united politically in one and the same sovereign national state is no older than the nineteenth century. In Europe, this identification of nation-hood with language has not been carried to extremes. Italy has not claimed to incorporate the Italian-speaking Swiss, nor Germany the German-speaking Swiss; and German-speaking Austrians have been as recalcitrant as the German-speaking Alsatians to being annexed to the German Reich. On the other hand, linguistic nationalism has prevailed in the Indo-Pakistani sub-continent since independence. The Bengali-speaking Muslim people of Bangla Desh have broken away from the Urdu-speaking Muslim people of Western Pakistan, in spite of their having the same non-Hindu religion. The Indian Union has been re-mapped internally into new provinces coinciding in area with the domains of the various local Indian languages.

What, then, is nationhood? Its basis is not really a common language or even a common political history; it is a common will to constitute a community whose members are united among themselves and are segregated from the rest of mankind. Nationhood, in this sense, is one of the most potent, and most disruptive, forces in a present-day world that seems likely to destroy itself if it refuses to unite on a global scale in which all the sectional nationhoods would be transcended.

9

People of Moscow
USSR

For these sailors and their wives, a summer's day off in Moscow means a picnic in Sokolniki Park. Children are cared for by a nursery.

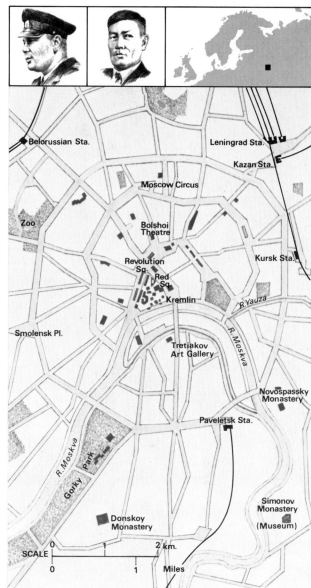

Moscow has not always been the capital city of Russia, and vast numbers of its inhabitants are first generation Muscovites, newcomers without roots in the city.

In the 14th century it was the capital: it had developed into a political and cultural center that consolidated the Russian lands into a strong, unified state. Then and until the reign of Peter the Great (1672-1725) Moscow was considered the 'third Rome', heir to the mighty center of the Roman Empire and to Constantinople. But during Peter the Great's reign it lost its status as capital. The tsar resolved that Russia should move culturally and politically closer to Europe, and St Petersburg – now Leningrad – assumed the role of first city. The élite of 11

At circus school in Moscow girls are taught the techniques of trapeze flying; in Russia, circuses flourish — in the west they decline.

Winter in Moscow is long and cold. Neither Napoleon nor Hitler could defeat the snow; but in Red Square, women simply brush it away.

St Petersburg (Petrograd) society avidly adopted French culture and language and rejected Moscow as an unfashionably rustic and embarrassingly Russian town. When the Bolsheviks reinstated Moscow as the capital city of Russia it was with the deliberate intention of isolating Russia from the west. They succeeded, for Moscow is unlike any other European capital city.

In 1920 after the Bolshevik revolution, there were just over one million inhabitants of Moscow. Today there are seven million. Yet Moscow heavily contributed to the 20 million Soviet dead in World War II and since 1936 a vast but unknown number were killed in the Stalinist terrors. Their disappearance was counterweighted by Stalin's crash program of industrialization, which brought people into Moscow from the furthest corners of the Soviet Union and rapidly increased the

The river Moskva, which runs through Moscow, ices up in the winter cold. For hardy swimmers, ice floes make convenient diving boards.

city's population. So a number of Moscow's people are not, in any historical or family sense, Muscovites. They are newcomers, or the children of newcomers. Most have come from villages or small towns and were peasants who sought the prosperity of life in a city. And Moscow, as capital of the Soviet Union, has drawn in people who may be from any of several major racial groups – Armenians, Georgians, and Azerbaijanis; Ukrainians, Moldavians and Byelorussians; Estonians, Latvians and Lithuanians; Turkmen and Uzbeks, Kirghiz, Tadjiks and Kazakhs – and many more lesser nationalities, including the hardpressed Jews and Tatars. Less than half the Soviet Union's people are Russian. But Moscow is unmistakably Russian.

People who have lived in villages for most of their lives tend to be unused to things which more established city-dwellers take for granted. Traffic may be something of which they are ignorant. In Moscow, people will cross a busy road as they might cross a village street. And indeed the streets of Moscow are surprisingly empty for a metropolis of people as well as cars. Moscow has less traffic than any major city of Europe, for the average family has no car. But there is some traffic; and when someone obliviously walks out in front of a truck or car or people stroll across a thoroughfare in gossiping clusters, lost to the world about them, angry drivers (who in the west would give vent to 'idiot!' or an obscenity) in Moscow simply shout 'peasant!'.

Authorities do their best to bring order to this confusion: police are strict on the pedestrian and driver alike. They will summon the miscreant jaywalker back to the pavement with a peremptory blast of their whistle, and direct him to the nearest official crossing. The driving test is, in theory, severe. It includes a searching examination on the mechanics of all internal combustion vehicles. But none of it induces the road sense that an urbanized westerner acquires from infancy.

Moscow is a huge city, with vast and complex industry, numerous railway terminals, three river ports, and four airports. The underground transport system is spectacular. It was initiated by Stalin as a major feature of the modernization program. Instead of grimy tunnels of rabbit warren complexity, the underground stations are vast cathedral-like halls, 40 feet high and decorated with murals and edifying inscriptions. The subway trains swish softly in and out on rubber wheels, and the passenger enjoys total comfort, with no jolts, no noise and no dirt. Moscow is a clean city. The problem of unemployment and city squalor have both been solved in one: every man or woman without a job is obligatorily employed as a sweeper or a window washer, and the city is spotless.

Since the revolution Muscovites have sacrificed much of their individual comfort and privilege in the name of progress. They are proud of the daunting monolithic blocks which are being raised in every quarter of Moscow.

13

Young Muscovites, like these university students in a 'guitar café', enjoy western jazz, once banned and still officially frowned on.

For the visit of President Nixon to Moscow, the building program was stepped up and the idiosyncratic corners of the city disappeared before the great gray filing-cabinets, the modern skyscrapers. The people in general cannot understand the fascination of the visitor from the west for all things ancient. At any murmur of regret at the passing of a lovely church or a statue, they will answer 'But it was useless. Look what we have in its place.' The need to attract foreign currency has made tourism an important industry – but the well-policed tourists are insistently shown only the inscrutable façades of new concrete monuments.

One foreign visitor – and how many have a story like this to tell—was staying in a block of flats which stood beside a modern motorway and looked out on a new fly-over. He discovered a small part of old Moscow: it lay behind his block, a maze of little lanes, many of them unmetalled, threading past old houses, some of mellowed brick and others of wood, and all set at odd and unexpected angles. There were trees all about and a flight of ancient stone steps led down to a small open place where a cow was tethered. Beyond this one of the free markets, which sold fruit and vegetables and flowers, looked out onto one of Moscow's tree-lined, grassy boulevards.

He walked through as if he had stepped into another world, another side of Moscow which had not forgotten the past and spoke of small beginnings and small communities. He paused to photograph one of the houses and was immediately approached by a passer-by who accused him of taking propaganda pictures of old buildings in order to spread it abroad that Russians were badly housed. He was angry at the thought of a visitor taking back memories and pictures of old houses when there was so much of the new to be seen.

This interfering is characteristic of Moscow people, especially of the older women. It is not unusual for a middle-aged woman to scold young mothers in the street or in the park for not having their children well wrapped up. It happens even in the height of summer, which can be very hot. You might easily think the people had arrived in the city only a few days before. But they will have been there for years, for a generation.

Muscovites care deeply for the welfare of their children. It is something quite natural to them as Russians, but as Soviet citizens it is also their duty. Children are essential to the solid Communist mystique, which is religious rather than political: a determined self-denial on behalf of a future that frail humans never quite deserve. For this future, Soviet citizens endure hardships and responsibilities, shortages and restrictions, which westerners would tolerate only in time of war or grave national crisis.

In Moscow family life is valued highly, possibly as a haven from city life, an intimate alternative to the grayness of an industrial and monolithic Moscow. It is all the more tragic that circumstances should weigh so heavily against family life. Despite the concentrated efforts to accommodate and encourage a swelling population the Muscovite's overwhelming anxiety is living space. Thousands of families or married couples share small flats with others. It is not only the industrial workers and government clerks in the vast urban tracts of shoddily constructed gray tower blocks and walk-up tenements, who find that when they marry they must live in just one room, sharing a kitchen, bathroom and wc with at least one other family; it is much the same for the scientists and professional people and the cream of Moscow's new young élite. The arrival of a second child can be a calamity. Overcrowding has kept the birth-rate down to one of the lowest in the world. Unfortunately the only reliable and widely available method of birth-control in the Soviet Union is abortion. The majority of women who have abortions are married.

Bringing up children is complicated by the fact that four fifths of Soviet women go out to work not only because the Communist ideology encourages them to do so, but out of sheer economic necessity. In a household where the husband earns an average salary it is the only way to make ends meet. Ordinary items like television sets and refrigerators can cost a worker three or four months' salary. Most families need two full salaries to live on. Although the state grants 56 days paid maternity leave, stipulates that a married woman's job must be held open for her for a year after the birth of the baby and provides day nurseries and crêches, there are still often insurmountable problems. A child of one year is young to be entrusted to a nursery. Most work schedules demand that parents must leave children at kindergartens before 8 am. Some children are virtually brought up by their grandmothers – if their grandmothers don't also go out to work. Part-time domestic help is almost impossible to come by in Moscow – doing somebody else's chores is regarded as demeaning. Many parents do not shower on their children all the devotion that they would wish.

There is also the holiday problem. An ordinary worker has one month's vacation. But most kindergartens and nurseries are open only until the end of May. Children under seven are not old enough to go to camp, and there are anyway insufficient camps for the older children who need them. So some parents take their holidays in separate months. This means that they never have a chance to get away together, no relief from the eternal problems of raising a family in a one-room flat. Family life, although cherished, is under perpetual strain. The Soviet divorce rate is the highest in the world.

It is the inclination of every Moscow parent to lavish on their children the best of everything. They dress them immaculately even if it means that they themselves must do without. Most of the toys on display in the huge Moscow store devoted entirely to children are less bizarre than those you find in children's stores in the west, but on any weekday children's shops have an

Big grey blocks, broad streets and sparse traffic (few Muscovitis can yet afford a private car) typify the new Moscow.

atmosphere of excitement which western shops only have at Christmas. (The Russian winter festival of the New Year has been largely displaced by the anniversary of the 'Great October Socialist Revolution' – the Bolshevik *coup* of 1917 – which falls on November 7.) The children hop about holding their parents' hands, as mischievous as children in any other place in the world.

Most children over ten years old will become members of the Party's Young Pioneers. They wear the red tie which symbolizes the revolution. As the children grow older they often join the youth movement, *Komsomol,* as an alternative to the Party. (Few Muscovites are full active party members.) This is generally apolitical, although under Communist auspices, and functions mainly as a social club organizing summer camps, concerts and dances for its young members, many of whom are students. The children learn their Communist ideology at school. Stalin's rigorous education program made great demands on school children, and until recently pupils in the upper schools were expected to do up to eight hours homework a night. In the autumn of 1970 the Council of Ministers of the USSR placed a legal limit on the amount of homework teachers could assign, ranging from one half hour in junior school to four hours for the seniors. Newspapers came out in support of the parents against those teachers who ignored this limit.

A great deal about children appears in the Moscow

Stalin thought chess was essential to every Russian's education. The game is now a national pastime and players regularly meet in Gorki Park.

press. Pretty children are a frequent choice for the covers of Soviet glossy magazines. There are innumerable articles about children's education, but like so much in the Soviet papers, statistics dominate everything: Russians have a consuming passion for statistics. It can be daunting to know the official figures on how many children attend crêches, kindergartens, schools, summer and winter holiday camps, houses of Young Pioneers, junior technical hobby centers, nature lovers' centers and other institutions.

At the Children's Theater, an imposing building close to the famous Bolshoi, there was recently a showing of *Peter Pan*, that traditionally Edwardian English middle-class play. How would Moscow actors and actresses perform this play? Would Captain Hook be portrayed as an archetypical capitalist thug? Would Peter Pan be the spirit of all Young Pioneers? Would Nana, the large nurse-maid dog, assume a Soviet guise? In fact the children were shown the play as it might be shown in London. Only Captain Hook was a little changed. In a

16

Old, pre-1917 Tsarist Moscow survives in unexpected corners but despite their snug atmosphere such homes are not sought after.

Women do the heavy work, men the skilled, in mending roads. Civilian trucks are painted grey in case the army needs them.

Despite attempts to reduce
religious influence, many
Russians attend mass — like
this at the last Novodevichi
monastery chapel still open.

On Easter day in Moscow the
'blessing of the bread' takes
place outside a church. Most
adherents to Russian Orthodox
Christianity are women.

17

Gravity and reserve – perhaps to be eased with vodka after the parade – mark the expressions of young officers in Moscow on May Day.

The military parade in Red Square is part of the May Day celebration, a show of strength and progress achieved since the 1917 revolution.

Russian rather than a Soviet way he had an air of Cossack banditry about him. Nevertheless, he was still unable to cope with the middle-class solidarity presented by the Darling family. The children adored every moment, right up to the last when Peter appealed for applause so that the fairy, Tinkerbell, should not die. The applause was deafening.

Despite the formal, unanimous society which the Soviet Union purports to be, Moscow people have much in common with people in other western cities. Daily they swarm to their factories in buses, trams and underground trains, pack vast stadiums to watch ice-hockey or football, or glue their eyes to television sets in the evenings. And just as there is more than one side of London and New York, there is more than one Moscow.

There is the official Moscow, which extends to every corner of the city's life. The bureaucracy is vastly ramified. It is rare for any of those processes of life that touch officialdom to be simpler than in the west. Divorce is one of these rare exceptions. Divorces are completed in a matter of minutes. A divorce case is performed before a judge with cold logic. The courtroom is bare; there is little emotion either offered or allowed. *Does the marriage work?* is what the judge wants to know. If it obviously does not, then a divorce is granted. Children are given to the care of either of the parents and the other must pay a fixed proportion of his or her income to help provide for the children. The rules are rigid, but also simple. Divorces tend to be – if not amicable – certainly unacrimonious affairs.

In Moscow's officially one-class society there are still signs of a social hierarchy. Russians are extremely rank- if not class-conscious, and everyone is placed physically and mentally in his own pigeon hole. There is an aristocracy of a sort, made up of politically powerful or scientifically eminent people. Today's aristocracy may have well-polished Chiaras, and chauffeurs to drive them, and occupy spacious flats in areas or buildings reserved specifically for them. In some cases, there is even a hierarchy within the block of flats: the more important

you are the nearer the sky you may live.

The privileged express their differences by their access to western styles and fashions; pop-music on the gramophones, the latest clothes, some of them manufactured in small quantities in the USSR but often brought in from the west by the few who are fortunate to travel. Immoralism, flaunted judiciously by some, is the mark of the privileged young: a disdain for accepted proprieties or for the puritanism of the patriotic dogma is represented by a vogue for pornography among the well-educated élite, fashionable because it is illegal. Even serious discussion of birth control or sex education is restricted in the Moscow press, or larded with euphemisms. Some young people in Moscow now have long hair. Ironically, they have got the idea from Soviet newsreels of riots among revolutionary and Marxist students in London and Paris.

There is a black market in Moscow which is tolerated if not actively encouraged by the state. Silk, nylon and ball-point pens are among the articles in great demand. A 19

(Left) Thousands throng Red Square by St Basil's cathedral on May Day with red banners reminiscent less of Marxist power than medieval panoply.

People of Moscow USSR

Science dominates Soviet
school curricula. Almost as
many Muscovite girls become
scientists as boys — and
later often run factories.

White for a bride is rare.
Muscovites marry in an office.
Divorce is easy — a brief
court hearing and a visit to
the Bureau of Statistics.

visitor might find himself approached – very politely – by a well-dressed man in the streets, and asked if he would like to sell his shirt. There is also a black money market, since the most interesting of Moscow's shops are the foreign currency stores, where a Muscovite can buy western clothes, leather goods and electrical gadgets as long as he can pay in dollars, yen, pounds or francs. No questions are asked on how he obtained this currency.

But the majority of Moscow's shops are dull and often stocked badly with little more than essential goods. One might have to queue for hours for some quite simple commodity – coffee or jam – in short supply. The chief store in Moscow is *Gum*, a vast building which extends for almost a quarter of a mile along one side of Red Square which it shares with the Kremlin. Inside the store there are many separate stalls selling a wide range of goods.

Among the mass of Muscovites, personal possessions are scant – a few sticks of furniture, one or at the most two changes of clothes for each of the two main seasons, the basic household utensils, a refrigerator for the better off, a radio and television, a cheap camera; and yet the ordinary Muscovite would be likely to say that he had never had it so good. It would be a frank and truthful statement. If he was old enough to remember the days before World War II, his answer would be all the more affirmative. In a material sense Muscovites are far better off than their grandfathers were seventy years ago. They give credit for this to the Party; some even include the discredited Stalin in their praise.

Many Muscovites equate their loyalty to the Party with patriotism toward Russia. Frequently this amounts to a crude chauvinism – and none of this would mean that they are Communists in any real sense. Russians – especially in the capital – support the ideology the way they support their football team. The glories and achievements of the Party are advertised the way consumer products are advertised in the west.

Not all Moscow newspapers are organs of party policy. Only *Pravda*, the organ of the Party Central Committee, and to a lesser degree, *Izvestia*, the government newspaper, are forums for top-level statements on foreign and domestic policy – which the more educated Muscovites are disposed to read between the lines. The rest of the proliferating newspapers and magazines reflect a wide range of activities and interests. They would be like western publications (which are not allowed in) were they not restricted in their content and in the opinions they express by what the authorities think permissible. Muscovites tend to avoid papers like *Pravda* and *Izvestia*. They are more likely to be seen consulting *Evening Moscow* to find out what's on at the movies or for the personal classified advertisements. The more liberal papers take up issues like education, the unmet consumer needs and the status of women, but within the permissible limits of course.

The position of women in Moscow society is ambivalent. A woman may well have a more exacting and better paid job than her husband, but she is expected to perform all the functions as mother, housekeeper and cook as well, almost invariably without domestic help. Officially there is no discrimination, but men tend to occupy the majority of managerial jobs while women often take over the heaviest labor. Whereas 75 per cent of Soviet doctors are women, there are few women surgeons or hospital directors. At an agricultural conference, Krushchev once remarked 'It turns out that it is the men who do the administering and the women who do the work.' As in the west the women's cause is being taken up by the press. One paper has suggested that women should be paid maternity benefit for several years after the birth of her child. Moscow with its low birth rate is in dire need of young citizens.

The Muscovite has had little chance to compare standards with those of the western world. The outsider recognizes the real restrictions on a Muscovite's freedom; the Muscovite himself is far less aware of them. Even in intellectual circles, contact with foreigners is made as difficult as possible for the Muscovite. Under Stalin it was a crime for a Soviet citizen to talk to a foreigner and the law has never been repealed. The visiting westerner has all his local staff and servants hand-picked for him by an official agency linked to the Secret Police.

But half a century of puritan dogma and endemic shortages have not reduced the Russians' innate love of food, drink, clothes and jollifications. Should the people of Moscow be suddenly presented with all the possibilities, good and bad, of the consumer society, they would tumble into them headlong like Gadarene swine – and Moscow would display all the features of New York and London within a matter of days. The stresses of life exist as much in Moscow as elsewhere. There are certain aspects of city life that neither Communism nor small communities within the conglomerate of Moscow can wipe out. The most outstanding of these is the desire which so many Muscovites have for getting drunk. Perhaps the desire is spurred by the restrictiveness, frustration and uniformity imposed by the political system; but it was always there in the depths of the introspective Slav temperament, bred in a climate of long snowbound winters and slow thaw which kept the great mass of Russians cooped up in their homes. To break out they drink vodka.

Muscovites do not seem just to go out for a drink; they go out intent on getting drunk. Statistics about drunkenness are not the kind of things that editors like to put in their newspapers, although recently there have been a few articles discussing the problem. But you can get a measure of it by strolling through the streets on any night between Friday and Monday morning. Muscovites are spectacular drunks – a few are merely befuddled, weaving their way homeward with slightly comic dignity; but most 21

Muscovites do the foxtrot to a steady loudspeaker beat in the grounds of the Exhibition of Achievements in Agriculture and Industry.

Vast manufacturing industries dominate Russia's economy, once farm-based. In Moscow, men and women share the shift work.

are uproarious, grasping at trees and lamp-posts with both hands, or lying spread-eagled, face downward and snoring across the footway. At night special police vans bring cargoes of helpless drunks to 'drying-out' stations where they are sluiced down and put to bed. In the morning they are fined summarily, though persistent offenders are often more heavily punished by stopping part of their wages. Increases in vodka and beer prices and limits of supplies are signals of the authorities' anxiety. But it still goes on. Moscow also has its 'skid-row,' frequented by real down-and-outs who cannot shrug off their alcoholism any more than the authorities can shrug off the problem. Moscow's 'skid-row' is close to Dzerzhinski Street named after the man who founded the Soviet secret police. There are more arrests for drunkenness in Moscow than for any other offence.

Even after years of officially godless Communism since 1917, Christianity is still a living force in Moscow. It is true that it is the old – especially old women – who attend the services at those few churches not converted into offices or museums, but increasing numbers of young people are now turning up as well. The official attitude, shared by many Muscovites, is to regard the priests as relics of the past when the expression 'a belly like a priest' was common among the poor peasants. Then the priests were regarded as being among the wealthier classes; even now they are thought by many to receive as much as five times what the average skilled worker earns.

There is, too, a definite revival of interest in all things Russian; especially things which have nothing to do with Communism or anything that has happened since 1917. Even intelligent people who are not remotely anti-Soviet, collect all kinds of old Russian objects and decorate their homes with them: articles of peasant manufacture, wooden carvings, spinning wheels, icons and crosses. They may be things that television archaeologists call 'ritual objects' but they do symbolize a revived consciousness of a Russian, rather than Soviet, identity. And to collectors they mean much more – they are a link with the past.

There is another side of Moscow. Beneath the grayness of their city, the people are warm and friendly and when their work is done for the day, or at weekends, they lead tranquil lives in snug little circles of family and friends. In this most public of cities, where the common good and common interest are expounded daily through all the agencies available to the government, most Muscovites spend their free days at home in a thoroughly private way. At weekends they retreat to a cosy inner world, and take food and drink with their friends over a private table. The facilities for public entertainment are sparsely scattered throughout the city; some of them are unusual, some improbable. But there are not many.

There are, for instance, few restaurants. There are no Italian or French restaurants and any place that is popular will inevitably be overcrowded: one may well

have to queue for an hour on the pavement outside. The Georgian restaurant is noisy and gay; the Berlin, which used to be called the Savoy until the early 1960s has baroque gilt ceilings and murals of naked but demure 18th century women. It has the air of a place where army officers would gather and women might spring forth and dance on the table. The Uzbekistan, which serves exotic food from that distant region of Russia, is always full of crowds of Russians in black and white skull-caps who come from romantic places like Samarkand, Bokhara and Tashkent.

In Moscow, however, families and relatives may often be split up. Members of families who have come from some far region – from Georgia, say, or Kazakhstan – will not be housed in the same place; it is, perhaps, a matter of policy that people are not grouped together on any other basis except profession. Resident foreigners live in special blocks; ballet and theater people in separate blocks of near-luxurious flats; and so too the Secret Police, members of the government, favored musicians, artists and writers. The official, bureaucratic Moscow decides where people should live. It can often conflict with the more personal, community life of Muscovites. 23

The Georgians
USSR

The Caucasus is the richest ethnic and cultural mosaic in the world. Here in the wild mountains that stand between the Caspian and Black Seas 68 quite distinct dialects are spoken. The looks of the inhabitants are almost as varied as their languages. For the last four thousand years the Causasus has witnessed unceasing human ebb and flow: wave upon wave of people invading, retreating or simply hiding. Sometimes this traffic has been peaceful. Carpet-weavers from Persia, silk-merchants from China, furriers from Russia, Greeks and Romans and Arabs, have harmoniously exchanged their goods at the crossroads of world culture. Islam and Christianity, as well as the age-old pagan beliefs of the isolated mountain people, have often violently conflicted. Yet sometimes the two great Mediterranean religions have happily existed together. Georgia, with frontiers extending from the Black Sea almost across to the Caspian, has been at the very hub of activity for thousands of years. Small wonder that the people have so rich a cultural heritage.

Nobody can fit the Georgians into a simple ethnic pattern. Their language is neither Indo-European, Turkic nor Semitic. The present Georgian nation must be a fusion of aboriginal inhabitants with immigrants who infiltrated the Caucasus from Asia Minor in remote antiquity. The Ossets in the north, descendants of the Scythian Alans chased by the Huns down from the Ukrainian plains, speak a language close to the present Iranians' Peshtu, but their culture has ties with Old Norse.

The name of Georgia itself varies from place to place. The people themselves call it Kartli after a mythical founder. The Greeks and Latins called it Iberia. The Armenians say Virk. Arabs call it Gurj – from which we get Georgia. So our name for the region has nothing to do with the people's patron saint St George.

The wealth and diversity of the Georgians' past certainly affects the people of today. There is evidence to suggest they were the first to make wine – a fact to be celebrated with pride. They still store young wine in clay pots by burying them in the earth. Identical pots 3,000 years old were unearthed recently and grape-pips found inside. Georgians are still proud horsemen – as they were in 79AD when they performed equestrian acrobatics before the Roman Emperor Vespasian. Huntsmen will tell you that the pheasant is so-called because it originated in Phasis (modern Poti). It was at Colchis, the present Georgian coastal land of Mingrelia, that Jason and his argonauts landed in search of the golden fleece: many of the mountain tribes still have their own versions of the legend.

Even quite recent architecture owes a debt to the past.

24

This Georgian is 120 years old and still going strong. Here he demonstrates a betrothal dance to his great grand-daughter.

Georgia has the highest mountains in the Soviet Union but in summer boasts one of the kindest climates in the world.

A shepherd tends the family's flocks. In the wild Georgian mountains many tribespeople are untouched by Communism and collectivization.

Like many Georgians this man — as his cap shows — is a Muslim. In the 4th century Georgia became Christian but Islam spread later.

The ages of these old buddies total 240 years. Regular physical activity, pure food and a stable emotional life are the secret of their longevity.

In the swampy areas near the Black Sea, wooden houses are still built on stilts. Mountain people adapted this technique and still build two-storied houses with comfortable top floors, open stables and pigsties below. Towers have always been common – the Svans up in the remote hills still place them overlooking the passes. Georgians also build 'lantern-vaulted' houses. The walls are erected in layers, each one tilting inwards till finally they meet at the pinnacle in a pyramid shape. This style was passed on to Georgian churches, which are frequently circular.

Most of the Georgians were fervent Christians and despite the victory of Communism many still are. St Nino, a slave woman, converted the Georgians as long ago as 330AD. St George readily became identified with the ancient moon god and was called White George (also, incidentally, the name of a nationalist movement of the 1930s). Many people of Asia Minor came to refer to the Georgians as 'Christians of the Girdle' after the tradition that St George bound up the dead dragon with a girdle.

Though there are pockets of Muslims in the regions of the Ajars and of the Abkhazians around Sukhumi, Georgians, led by the Bagration family for over a thousand years, were usually successful in warding off the Muslims. The royal family's coat of arms focused on a seamless shirt, like the one Christ wore on the cross, which symbolized the Bagration claim of descent from David and Solomon and their consequent blood-relationship with the Savior. The Georgian Church, bolstered by its antiquity, has developed strongly held dogmas not shared by other churches. For example Georgian Christians believe that the Creation took place in exactly 5604BC.

The Church was the driving force behind the growth of Georgian art and literature. By 500AD the priests had 27

All five councillors in the village of Lyxny in the high Caucasus are over a hundred years old. The Russian Lenin (this statue) died at 56.

All five councillors in the village of Lyxny in the high Caucasus are over a hundred years old. The Russian Lenin (this statue) died at 56.

ghomi, a paste that comes from millet. Eating habits vary from region to region.

It is a mistake to think of the Georgians as a totally integrated people. Undoubtedly they have been drawn together by religion, common enemies and a common language. But it is only during the Soviet era that some of the mountain tribes have been included in the nation of Georgia. Many of them still cling to the language and habits of their separate ancestors. The Ossets even have their own autonomous republic which is incorporated in Georgia. They can still keep their traditional tough practices: even today, adulteresses may have their ears and noses cut off. Both the wild Khevsurs and the Svans, are strictly endogamous – they try if possible to marry first cousins. They also follow a custom which dictates that after marriage the couple must separate for a year. Many of the tribes of the mountains also forbid brides to bear children till after they have been married for three years. The Pshavs allow a maximum of three children per couple. Many mountain peoples pray that their wives will bear boys: they mourn a girl's birth.

The climate of Georgia is almost as varied as the people. If you take a train from the Black Sea port of Batumi, you will find the scenery tropical and the air humid. Many exotic plants grow wild beside the railway. As well as fields full of magnolia and blue hydrangea, there are rice fields and, as you go east, cotton fields. Climbing away from the coastal region, you will see more and more orchards rich with peaches and apples. As you pass through the land of the Svans you see birches and rhododendrons. In central Georgia, where the land slopes less steeply, there are citrus plantations. Tbilisi itself is famous for its warm springs. In the last century Russian aristocrats from Moscow would bring consumptive relatives and friends to take cures at the waters. East of Tbilisi the hills even out into a rolling plain covered in vineyards and tobacco plantations.

The physical types are as varied. The Ossets are often tall and blond. The people from around Tbilisi are usually stocky and dark, though red-heads are quite common. The aquiline noses of many of the inhabitants show Armenian influence. Slit eyes, lank black hair and yellowish skin suggest the blood of Kalmuks from the north Caucasus where mongol remnants still survive.

Yet travelers report a consistent hospitality and warmth throughout Georgia. Common influences – which have resulted in cultural similarities among the inhabitants as well as a direct mingling of their blood – have not turned them into one people. Despite the grief that some mountain tribes feel when a girl is born, a feature common to almost all Georgian groups is the cult of women. Queen Tamar is revered by all Georgians for her merciful 11th century rule. St Nino is admired by Muslims as well as Christians. It is authoritatively said that one of the chief reasons why Georgia was by and large spared the worst excesses of the Stalinist campaign against the

developed an alphabet of their own. A 'Warriors' alphabet' followed – itself quite different. Then the Georgians invented their own totally separate system of musical notation.

The Georgians love music of all kinds – not merely Church tunes, or the chants of the Gregorians from neighboring Armenia. The Mountain-Jews (or Judaeo-Tats) have their own style; so do the pagans. Throughout Georgia people enjoy the sounds of the flute, lute, drums and cymbals. Bagpipes and mandolines are played as well.

The universal time for playing is after a few drinks. *Chacha* (or grape-vodka) is the favorite. It comes at all times of the day. There is tea for abstainers, but they are few. Yogurt and fruit juices are popular, especially in the hills. Melons, oranges and mandarins are often added to a diet of goat or chicken strongly spiced with peppers or heavily seasoned with garlic. In some parts a doughy maizemeal called *mameliga* is eaten. In others they prefer

28

Although mountain people pray for the birth of a boy and lament when a girl is born, women are greatly revered.

Church was that Stalin himself (who was a Georgian) was frightened of his staunchly Christian mother.

A feature of life in Georgia is its unusual length. Georgians probably live longer on average than any other people on the earth. No topic tends to be more obscured by vanity and deceit than old age. Extreme claims are often made on behalf of the very aged, rather than by them. It has been suggested that the great age professed by many Georgian men results from attempts when they were younger to avoid military service by assuming the identities of older men. Certainly the Georgians in Tsarist times were lax about registering births. The most reliably pedigreed group of people in the world, the British peerage, has after ten centuries produced only one peer who has reached even his hundredth birthday. Nevertheless, careful examination has shown that the Georgians do indeed have a large number of centenarians – at Sukhumi on the Black Sea a full-blooded orchestra, composed entirely of men of over a hundred, strikes up twice a year. And they apparently play in tune.

The old men of Georgia live in a healthy climate usually at a high altitude. They eat a lot of fruit. But they drink and smoke quite happily. Some are vegetarians, some are not. They are certainly not mollycoddled. Many of them ride horses till well past their hundredth year; some even play the rough game of Georgian polo. It is true that their diet is generally a good one but the secret of old age is more psychological than one of diet.

Old Georgians are of above average intelligence, according to the recent survey by the Tbilisi gereontologist Dr Pitskelauri. Emotionally they are remarkably stable. They have large families and enjoy strong family ties, temperance and plenty of sleep. They are often manual workers. They live lives of extreme regularity. Above all they are insulated from social upheaval – most of the very old Georgians live in remote hill villages. They lead physically vigorous lives free from urban strain. Although women have a three times better chance of passing 80, men outnumber women by three to one past the 100 mark.

It is not surprising that the Georgians have learnt to live long. They have had to learn to live in many ways. They have come to terms over the ages with climate, culture and race. In 1801 Georgia was conquered by the Russians. The Soviets took over where the Tsarists left off. But even though they are so diverse a collection of people, the Georgians are still as nationalistic as ever. Their intermingling has enriched and united more than it has disrupted.

29

Norsemen
Scandinavia

Father and sons continue the
ancient Viking techniques in
Norway's traditional means
of earning a living in winter
—boatbuilding.

H undreds of sea-chasms, jutting inland, make up Norway's 21,000 kilometer coastline. The coastal mountains rise straight out of the sea. Only some 14.000 years ago did the glaciers of the last Ice Age recede. It was then that stone-age man moved forth from Jutland and Germany to settle along the fjords.

Norway's mountainous spine concedes only the occasional patch of arable land. A mere twentieth of Norway's entire area can be cultivated. On the southern coast around Oslo and along the great valley of Gud- 31 bransdal there are large-scale grain and dairy operations. But small subsistence farms predominate in the west and north.

This is where the boatbuilders live. The boatbuilders uphold a Viking tradition that has almost died. They usually live on farms of about 40 acres which spread out along the fjords. Most of them devote themselves to farming, but they exploit sea and forest as well as pastureland. They live in clusters of small-holdings. When they want the hay brought in or a barn raised or repaired, everyone from the hamlet lends a hand. But for the normal workload the farmers tend to rely on their sons.

When winter comes, the boatbuilders – a dwindling breed – set off into the forest to fell fir for the traditional work of winter. Boatbuilding is profitable, but it is also a labor of love. Fathers teach their sons how to build the boats and instil in them a love of the craft, handed down from father to son since the days of the Vikings.

Like the Viking warrior boats, with their huge carved prows, that descended on Europe from the north between 800 and 1100 AD, the boats built today are about 22 feet long. Helped by his sons the craftsman builds the boat strake by strake from the keel. The keel was a revolutionary Viking invention. Starting with the bow-stem, shaped by axe from the naturally strong junction of a fir's trunk and runner-root, the sturdy craft takes form in the family barn which in winter becomes a boat-shop. The first strake is riveted to the keel. With a hand-sized pattern the hull's gracefully curving lines are set as the next two strakes are put in place. Only when these first three strakes are finished does the elegant pea-pod form receive slender ribs, more to give shape and support the seats than as a source of strength.

Farmers who fish for the family usually purchase the fjord-boats along Norway's coast. But of the dozen boats each builder makes in a season, a few are shipped off to city dwellers. More and more of them appreciate the value of a traditional wooden boat, as a symbol of retreat from their urban world.

The life of the boat-builder farmers is impressively self-sufficient. The mother of the house bakes the family bread weekly, kneading the dough in a wooden trough – a close relation of the kneading trough found in 1903 when a Viking burial ship was excavated nearby. She also dries and salts the cod and herring fished by her husband. Home-made jams of forest-gathered berries are the *pièce de résistance* of the day's two cold meals of bread, cheese, eggs and cured meat. The one hot meal is usually eaten at noon, but coffee and sweet cakes are always at hand for the family and visitors. The household tasks pile up as winter's darkness culminates in the traditional Yuletide gathering, which was held long before Christianity arrived in Norway 1,000 years ago. The father of the house brews plenty of strong dark beer. Pigs are slaughtered and blood pudding, sausage, pigs'

head cheese and pickled pigs feet are prepared. Hams are salted, smoked and stored for the coming year. They will be eaten with home-grown cabbages, potatoes, turnips and carrots stacked away in the dark, frost-free cellar below the farmer's two-storey white house.

The fjord-side boatbuilders are rarely enticed to the few large towns along the Norwegian coast. They feel protected by the mountains that barrier the fjord. Many of the men have lived away from the fjords, but they all come home in the end. The farm is the pivot of their life.

Although only one son inherits the farm, as ordained by ancient Norse law, he pays the others proportionately for the privilege of inheritance. The Norwegian government, in turn, backs the small fjord farms with subsidies, convinced of the farm's importance to Norway's national character, and wants to ensure the survival of small farming families despite the Common Market regulations on free agricultural competition.

Viking traditions persist elsewhere in Scandinavia. Norway's neighbor Sweden is sometimes seen as the prototype of the world to come. It has been the first to plan urban complexes; has pioneered a social welfare system that surrounds Swedes with State security. Perhaps as a counter-balance, the Swede attaches great importance to sport. But it is not only modernized sports like skiing, which originated in the Scandinavian Iron Age, that captivate the Swede.

On the Swedish island of Gotland, in the middle of the Baltic Sea, the people still play the ancient Viking games. Every summer competitors flock to the sport Olympiad. They play *Varpkastning,* a cross between discus throwing and horse-shoe pitching. The player hurls his four kilo *varpa* twenty meters to a stake. The women are let off with casting a half-weight *varpa* fifteen meters.

The great challenge to strength is the *stangstot.* Contestants lift a log to the vertical, then toss it. The Scots will concede their fabled caber toss with its running throw is descended from this sport, probably brought to Scotland, by colonizing Vikings. Another Viking challenge, now internationally contested, is the hammer toss, which started as the throwing of 'Thor's hammer.'

Gotlanders live apart from mainland Sweden on their island limestone plateau, 250 miles around. The harbor city of Visby, its turreted walls still encircling a medieval city of narrow cobbled streets and tiny houses, contrasts with the sheer walls of modern Swedish architecture. 92 of Gotland's 93 churches were established by 1400 AD when the island was supreme in the trade of the Baltic. Norse inscriptions tell that Gotlanders were among the Vikings who voyaged to the great rivers of Russia and traded with Slav and Arab merchants at Kiev on the Dnieper and Bulgar on the Volga, offering them furs, amber and slaves. Gotlanders also erected picture stones – nearly 300 of them. On these slabs, some over six feet high, the gods and legends of the Norsemen still parade before the descendants of those who cherished them.

A Gotlander spits on his *varpa* for luck. *Varpkastning*, is an ancient Viking sport similar to discus throwing and horseshoe pitching.

A lady *Varpkastning* contestant throws her 2-kilo *varpa* 15 meters, but the men are expected to throw 4-kilo *varpas* 20 meters.

The ancient Viking contest of manly strength, *stångstöt* — log-throwing — was introduced by Vikings to the Scots who still 'toss the caber.'

Where the runner root joins the main trunk of the Norwegian fir is a natural boat keel — already roughly shaped and pre-stressed.

In bigger versions of boats built on this design Vikings adventured as far as 'Vineland' (America), settled in Iceland and dominated Europe's coastlands.

Islanders of Karpathos
Greece

Gold coins — the family
heirlooms — and other finery
display this young maiden's
dowry. Once married she will
dress like her companion.

SÁRIA

SCALE

| 0 | 4 | 8 km. |
| 0 | 4 | Miles |

Olympos•

KÁRPATHOS

MEDITERRANEAN
SEA

Pigádhia

Menetai

At a time when new and external influences are devitalizing the musical folk heritage of many cultures, the musical traditions of the people of the village of Olympos on the island of Karpathos remain strong, unbroken and relatively unaffected. The creativity of the people of Olympos, or Elympítes as they are called, 35

Islanders of Karpathos Greece

Olympos, in the harsh north of Karpathos, was built out of sight of pirates. Only a dirt road connects it to the coast.

A lute (left) and a lira, the traditional combination of instruments, are played at a village wedding feast. Sometimes bagpipes are added.

After the days of Lenten
abstinence the villagers
gather for an Easter Tuesday
feast and dancing in the
village square.

still finds expression through music and dancing. And
the socio-religious life of the community which sustains
the music, is still intact—although it is under increasing
strain. Olympos gives a unique chance to observe a way
of life that has remained unaltered for centuries. From
such roots eastern Mediterranean island culture has
sprung.

The village of Olympos is at the northern end of
Karpathos, one of the Dodecanese group of Greece. It
has, according to the 1971 census, a population of 500;
Diafani, its port, has another 300 inhabitants. It was
probably settled in the 10th century in the Byzantine
period after one of the periodic incidents of devastation
by pirates of an earlier population on their part of the
island. Judging from the Elympítes' distinctive dialect
their ancestors were not of the same stock as the Greeks
who inhabited the rest of the island either before or after
they came there.

The site of the village was obviously chosen for its
inaccessibility: the solid, whitewashed, flat-roofed stone
and mortar houses of the village, are built into the sides
of the mountain. Olympos is perched like an eyrie from
which all approaches to the village can be viewed. There
are only two feasible ways of getting there from the other
nine villages of the island to the south and from the

world outside – by a long, difficult footpath, or by sea
from the village's port, Diafani.

Houses are built on slopes so steep that their floors are
level with the roofs of the houses below. The houses have
one all-purpose room, with only one window. In the
older houses, the cooking hearth was built into the wall
of this same room. Newer houses have a small kitchen
next door.

The only furnishings are a table and some chairs, a
long storage bench and a few cabinets built into the wall,
and a raised two-level wooden platform, usually along
the whole wall opposite the entrance to the room. The
hollow space beneath the platform, which often extends
into the rock of the mountain, is a kind of larder: grain,
flour, olive oil, cheeses and other foods are stored there.
The family sleep together on top of the platform; every
morning the bedding is neatly rolled and stacked at the
back. Hung from the vertical and horizontal carved rails
of the platform are the vividly colored handwoven cloths
made for her dowry by the woman of the house. The only
other decoration in this rather severe room are the rows
of porcelain and ceramic plates and pitchers hung high
along the walls, and a big, hanging mirror in a carved,
dark wooden frame.

Music and dancing are important for the Elympítes 37

The cobbler makes all the villagers' boots and shoes including the high boots the women wear. He also plays the bagpipes.

not only on festive occasions but also in everyday life. Young men continue to learn to play the traditional instruments: the *lyra* – a three-string instrument which they play with a bow strung with bells, the *laouto* – a long-necked lute which they strum with a plectrum, and the *tsambouna* – the shrill goat-skin bagpipe of the island.

When the men gather in the two or three coffee houses off the square of the village playing cards or talking, one of them will pick up a *lyra* and play, either for the benefit of his companions or for the entire café. A *laouto* player may join in. And then one of the instrumentalists or another man will start to sing a *tavla* (table) song. It will be one of many that are in the collective memory of the villagers. Or the singer may prefer to improvise and express his feelings of the moment. Or he may greet an old friend who has just arrived by singing rhymed distichs (couplets) to one of the melodies in his repertoire. The phrasing of the words is long and extended, and every now and then a chorus of voices will repeat some part of the distich.

Music also pervades the islanders' religious life – not least, of course, the marriage ceremony. Throughout the evening and the night following the ceremony, the village bride sits raised on a platform with her bridesmaids and the other women. There she is served, while at long tables in the room below the groom and the men feast, and then sing the traditional marriage songs to the accompaniment of their instruments. In the morning the bride descends from the platform to serve first her father-in-law and then all the other men with drinks and sweets; each in turn sings to her, expressing his own emotions and extolling her in improvised rhymed distichs that are copied in a notebook by one of her attendants on the platform.

This notebook is for the bride to keep – but she and her family and guests will already have committed the good distichs and the identity of their creators to memory.

The *kavai* is the women's principal costume. This is a blue, home-woven, long-sleeved coat worn over a white, shirt-like garment, and long bloomers tucked into boots, with a belt and apron made of bought material, and kerchief tied so as to hide all the hair except the ends of the plaits which hang down the back. The women's hands become deep blue from handling the yarn with which they weave the cloth for the *kavai*. Little girls wear simple, cotton print frocks and babies – both boys and girls – wear bright satin dresses. On festive occasions young unmarried women wear dresses of sumptuous, purchased material with a bib of gold coins to display their dowry.

Only a few of the very old men still dress in the traditional breeches and jacket made of the same blue cloth as the *kavai*. Most wear plain leather boots and ordinary European clothes.

Most of the villagers are dark-eyed, olive-skinned and dark-haired and are their own ideal of beauty. They are

38

The whole village is whitewashed for Easter. Besides making it look clean the lime in the wash acts as a disinfectant.

Flour is unloaded at the
tiny port of Olympos.
Supplies are carried up to
the village by donkey or jeep
on the narrow, winding road.

(Above) Children who do well
in their 6 years at the
village school, board in a
village in the south and
attend the high school there.

(Center) The north wind
blows strongly in the Greek
islands. Windmills are still
used for grinding wheat
into flour.

39

Islanders of Karpathos Greece

Elympíte homes have neither electricity nor running water. The family wash is done in a pool near the main spring of the village.

An Elympíte shepherd wears the traditional homespun breeches and jacket and hand-made leather boots.

usually slender and stand very straight. Slenderness is valued as an indication of industriousness and strength of character.

By the traditional system of inheritance the eldest son received when he married all his father's property and goods through the male line; and the eldest daughter received her mother's property through the female line. This system – now less strictly adhered to – meant that land holdings in the village were unequal. The restless, more enterprising small landowners went off in groups, leaving the village and their families, to work under contract as builders in the neighboring islands, or in Greek settlements along the coast of Asia Minor. Some went as far as Persia, North Africa and South America. They would stay away for years. But the men whose jobs were less far afield would leave home regularly in the spring after Easter and return around Christmas. When the travelers returned to the village, they would purchase additional land. Now the pattern of emigration is more in line with the rest of Greece: whole families leave for the United States, Canada and Australia; or husbands go off alone or with their wives to work temporarily in the factories of western Europe. When the mother is away, elderly grandmothers care for the children.

But usually only the man is absent from the younger families. The wife then assumes total responsibility for her children and for running the household. In the daily routine, the domestic chores and cooking are done quickly and efficiently, without the conveniences of electricity and running water. But the outside activities – fetching water, doing the laundry at the spring, tending the livestock, baking the bread for the week every Saturday, and even harvesting and olive picking – are arduous and time consuming. The farm work is gruelling, as it is done over great distances and in difficult mountainous terrain. The wife relies on her mother, sometimes her mother-in-law, and her children for help. Elympítes have mainly been farmers and shepherds. Unlike some of the nearby islanders, they have not gone to sea as fishermen, sponge divers, or merchant seamen. The land they cultivate is rich, productive and level – albeit some distance from the village. It yields grain, vegetables and grapes – and requires no watering. There are also the olive trees to cultivate and harvest. During the olive picking the villagers do not go home every evening but stay in houses grouped together in special settlements near the olive groves. The terraces, carefully cut long ago into the sides of the nearby vertical mountains in such a way that the earth would not be carried away by the rains, have now been abandoned. Seasonal greens and vegetables are grown in the irrigated valley beneath the village.

The seven or eight shepherds of the village herd their sheep and goats over a large area of the mountains. As this is a family enterprise – the wife and children help not only in the herding but also in the milking and cheese-

Islanders of Karpathos Greece

Elympíte women prepare dough for the Easter cheese cakes. Easter coincides with plenty of sheep's and goat's milk and thus lots of cheese.

A woman works colored yarns into a floral design on a piece of cloth being loomed in her house. Looms are built in the village.

On the steep hillsides only small patches of land are cultivated around the fig trees. This woman attacks her plot with a mattock.

Islanders of Karpathos Greece

Women dye eggs for the village's most important festival — Easter. Once they only dyed them red but now they are done in many colors.

Basil and flowers decorate the *epitaphios*, representing Christ's tomb, for the Good Friday service. Later they are shared out.

Easter cakes — *koulouria* — decorated with colored eggs are carried into the house from a communal out-door oven.

Women light *kantilia* — vigil lights — at the cemetery in Easter week. After prayers the cakes are shared with bystanders.

At the Orthodox cemetery church of Agios Jiannis (St John) in Olympos, the bell is rung after the death of a villager.

making – whole families are away from the village over long periods of time.

The Elympítes value education highly. Children who do well in their village grade school are sent in their early teens to the only high school on the island which is in a village in the south. The child rents a room with a family where, because of limited funds, he does his own cooking and washing. Occasionally a basket of food will arrive from home. The only time during the school year when the children from Olympos return to their village is at Easter. Usually, this is a season of unsettled weather; boat services are irregular and the children sometimes have to walk for twelve or more hours in single file along the narrow, tricky footpath to their village.

The annual cycle of religious holidays gives everybody more opportunities to join in festivities, which always culminate in singing and dancing by both men and women. Most popular are saints' days which fall at times of the year when people can gather outdoors to honor the Saint – at *Panegyria*, festivals universal to all Greece.

The cycle of holidays starts with Easter. Other festivals are scattered throughout late spring and early summer; but the height of the *Panegyria* is 15 August, the day of the Assumption of the Virgin. Then on 29 August the principal church of the village celebrates the festival of St John traditionally associated throughout rural Greece with the deliverance of the people from malaria by his saintly intervention. On 8 September a little outlying chapel near one of the two principal springs of the village celebrates the birthday of the Virgin.

The Easter festivities follow a long interval of fasting and self-denial by the villagers. Church and home activities during Easter week in Olympos are essentially no different from those in other Greek villages, except for the morning service on Good Friday and the entire day of festivities on the Tuesday after Easter. These are celebrated in a unique way in Olympos. At the church on Good Friday morning, women who have been bereaved by the death of members of their families mourn and sing laments before the *Epitaphios* (the flower decorated bier of Christ). Their songs of loss and their gestures of total despair as they pull at the loosened braids of their hair bring a response of sobs from women and men alike.

Once the priest at the Easter Eve midnight service has proclaimed the tidings of Christ's Resurrection and the promise of eternal life through death, the villagers, old and young alike, impatiently await the coming Tuesday. Early on Tuesday morning there is a procession of Byzantine splendor – headed by the priest in rich brocade vestments followed by the entire population of the village all dressed up in their best clothes – in which strong young men carry on their shoulders the large icons of the Virgin, Christ, St John the Baptist, and St John the Evangelist out from the village to a succession of places. The procession stops at little chapels on the mountain slopes outside the village, where the priest

reads prayers for the deliverance of the people from pestilence, famine, earthquakes and floods. There is a longer stop at St John the Baptist's cemetery where prayers are said at each of the graves, and food served from on top of the grave is an affirmation of the un-interrupted unity of the dead with the living. Later at the spring of the 'Charitable Virgin' where the face of the Virgin on the icon is washed, prayers are said for the intervention of the mother of Christ so that the life-giving spring may be kept running. Then the icons are carried back to the church in the village. This is the time for men and women, young and old, and the children too, to start the long line of dancing which sometimes continues for thirty-two hours without a break. Out in the fresh spring air all the people of Olympos express through their dancing and singing their own affirmation of life. 43

In accordance with the laws of the Greek Orthodox Church. this Elympíte child will be baptized by total immersion in the font.

Europe's Gypsies and the Camargue festival

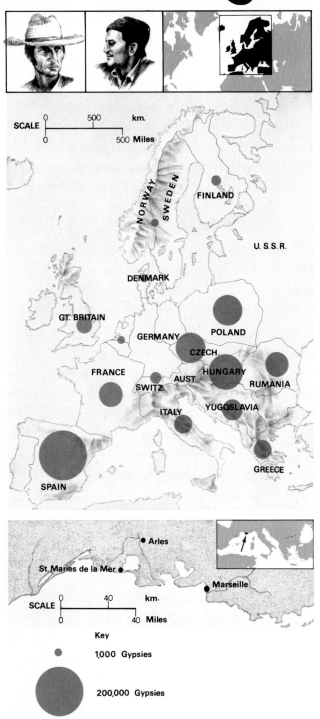

SCALE 0 — 500 km.
0 — 500 Miles

NORWAY
SWEDEN
FINLAND
U.S.S.R.
DENMARK
GT. BRITAIN
GERMANY POLAND
CZECH.
FRANCE HUNGARY
SWITZ. AUST. RUMANIA
ITALY YUGOSLAVIA
GREECE
SPAIN

• Arles
St. Maries de la Mer •
• Marseille

SCALE 0 — 40 km.
0 — 40 Miles

Key

● 1,000 Gypsies

● 200,000 Gypsies

In the south of France the Camargue lies like a stretch of waste land, parched and torn by mistral winds in summer and whipped and flooded by rains in the winter. The marshes are everywhere and the Rhône empties into the sea through a maze of shallow deltas. The Camargue is possessed by an air of mystery, haunted

44

Every year Gypsies from all over Europe gather in the Camargue (bottom map) to mark the legend of the two holy Marys. The big map shows Gypsy numbers.

45

At the Gypsy festival of
Saintes Maries de la Mer, the
effigy of St Mary (one of the
two Marys present at Christ's
death) is borne seawards.

Gypsies, followed by mounted cowboys from the Camargue, come down to the sea shore where, legend tells, the two Marys first landed in France.

by an ancient, dark past. Like the Gypsies themselves, who make an annual pilgrimage to Saintes-Maries-de-la-Mer in the Camargue, this country does not seem a part of Europe – it is a steppe, a barren marsh, a watered desert.

In May, when the grasses and reeds begin to wither and the marshes dry up and crack in the heat, the Gypsies come to celebrate the 500 year-old legend of the two holy Marys. Here, at the village of Saintes-Maries, the Gypsy Sara first greeted the Marys as they landed on their pilgrimage to France. Sara was baptised in the Christian faith – and the Gypsy worship of her memory has been continuous since that time. They come to the village church, and in the crypt they stand before their shrine to Sara, a simple black effigy and an altar.

From across France the *Gitanes* (Gypsies) gather in their thousands for the vigil at the shrine of their lady, Sara. But the vigil is disrupted by the tourists who flock to watch them at their dances and singing. Gypsy women's brightly colored dresses writhe to the sound of flamenco guitars and harsh songs; they clap hands and tap their feet in a frenzy of rhythm. The Gypsies are brash; in their inimitable nomad way they also take advantage of their audience. It is like a sly warfare. The mysticism of the occasion is quickly lost as Gypsy orthodoxy (or that which is expected of them) takes over. They pounce and claw and flutter in their bright rags. The watching tourists, smiling half with fear, half entranced, seek out the dishonesty they expect; they cast around for the vagabonds, the thieves, the beggars and the weavers of spells. These are things they have heard about Gypsies and for this reason they are fascinated by them. They are poles apart, the 'civilized' Frenchmen and the nomadic Gypsies – and unlike poles attract. This festival draws all together.

Nobody knows exactly where the Gypsies came from. There is confusion, too, about who exactly the Gypsies are. But what is certain is that the Gypsies are nomads. There is no archaeological evidence of the pattern of their wanderings: no buildings, no monuments, no tablets, no graves. But Gypsies are found in almost every country of the world. There are possibly as many as two million scattered in small groups all over Europe from the USSR to Ireland.

Only the evidence of language, legend and literature indicates that they originated from India. When exactly they left India, and in what circumstances, is not known. Philologists, on the evidence of linguistic evolution, believe they could not have left before AD 1000. Others believe they may have left much earlier: Homer wrote about a group of people called the *Sinti* – believed to be one of the earliest branches of the Gypsy race in India, who by tradition were among the first to travel westward.

Certainly, if hard evidence is lacking, there is much to suggest that they were outside India long before AD 1000. The Persian poet Firdusi tells us that in about AD 420

Prince Bahram of Persia imported ten thousand nomad musicians of both sexes from India. The Arabian historian Hamza of Isfahan, writing half a century earlier than Firdusi confirms this story. He calls them the *Zott,* which is the modern *Jat,* one of a number of Arabic words for Gypsy.

The Gypsy word for men is *Rom* in Europe, *Lom* in America, and *Dom* in Persia and Syria. The Gypsies of modern India too are called *Dom.* And this translated from modern Hindu, is 'itinerant musician: a man of low caste who gains his living by singing and dancing.'

The year 1417 is the widely accepted date for the Gypsies' first appearance in Europe, when a large number descended upon Lüneburg in Germany. But as they carried letters of recommendation from the King of Hungary, they must obviously have travelled through that country. And their leaders, their 'dukes,' bore good Christian names like Andrew, Michael and Thomas, indicating long familiarity with Christian lands.

We now know that the Gypsies were present in Europe for many years before that appearance in 1417 in Germany; possibly from AD 855. They clearly spent much time in Greece before spreading westwards over Europe, for Greek words occur in all the European Gypsy dialects, including Welsh and English.

In any language there is of course a two-way traffic in words. The Gypsy picks up some words of the country in which he lives or travels and loans to it some of his own. Thus the English word *chores* is the Gypsy word for *work* or *job.* Two other Gypsy words incorporated into normal English speech are *cosh* and *trash. Cosh* means a *heavy stick. Trash* is Romanes for *fright;* the man who is frightened or a coward is trash – a worthless creature.

The first official record of Gypsies in Great Britain was

Effigies of the two Marys are
carried into the sea — where
2,000 years ago they are
believed to have landed —
and are immersed thrice.

Gypsies touch the image of
St Sara, the Black Virgin,
with cloth and silk kerchiefs.
Sara was the first Gypsy to
be baptized by the Marys.

Europe's Gypsies and the Camargue festival

Camargue cowboys gather
round to watch the ritual
immersion of the two Marys.
This rite is a blessing of the
sea—and a ritual of purification.

Gypsies are thought to have
originated in India before
their wanderings across
Europe. Their faces and their
language appear un-European.

Tobacco, smoked or chewed, is a favorite Gypsy pleasure. Old women constantly smoke tobacco or dried leaves in roughly fashioned pipes.

in Scotland in 1505. It occurs in the Lord High Treasurer's accounts and is very short: *1505, April 22. Item to the Egyptians be the King's command VII lib.* It seems to be generally accepted that this £7, a considerable sum, was payment for some form of entertainment. It is more likely that it was a charitable contribution to 'pilgrims.' There is also strong circumstantial evidence for the presence of Gypsies in the British Isles even earlier—in Wales, around 1430 and in Scotland and northern England ten years later. But these were small groups, anxious not to be noticed.

For in July of the same year we find the king James IV, writing to his uncle, the king of Denmark commending to him 'Anthony Gagino, a Lord of Little Egypt' who with his retinue had reached Scotland a few months earlier 'during a pilgrimage through the Christian world, undertaken at the command of the Apostolic See.'

The original story, first officially recorded in 1420 at Deventer in the Netherlands, was rather different. This told how the 'Lord Andrew, Duke of Little Egypt,' with his retinue of 'one hundred persons and forty horses' had been driven from his country because he had embraced the Christian faith. The story so touched the City Fathers that they subscribed a large sum of money to help the distressed nobleman on his way.

Lord Andrew's way then led him to northern Italy to Bologna. He arrived there in 1422 with his retinue of 'two hundred persons, men, women and children, and many horses.' He told the same story, but now he had a wife, who 'could foretell what would happen to a person during his life, as well as what was interesting in the present, how many children would be born, whether a woman was good or bad, and other things.' This seems to be the first official reference to a Gypsy fortune-teller. Lord Andrew's wife was a great success; so great a success that the City Fathers finally felt impelled to pay the band to leave. The price was heavy.

Five years later in 1427 a Gypsy band of one hundred and twenty led by a duke and an earl arrived in Paris. The story was the same: that they had been driven from Lower Egypt because they had embraced the Christian faith. The chronicler is at pains to describe them. They were dark-skinned, the women wore long black skirts of a coarse material, but above the skirt bright colors. Their ears were pierced and 'in each a silver ring, or two in each.' But what struck him most was that 'there were witches in their company who looked into people's hands and told what had happened to them, or would happen. And while they were speaking to folks by magic or otherwise, or by the enemy in hell, or by dexterity and skill, it was said they emptied people's purses and put into theirs. But in truth I went there three or four times to speak to them, but I never perceived that I lost a penny.'

What is beyond question is that the public were so keen to have their fortunes told that they came to Paris from miles around. Particularly on Sundays – with the result that the churches began to empty, 'so that the

Gypsy children are darlings of the group. They are allowed complete freedom throughout the camp and amuse themselves without any toys.

'Always help brothers; never harm brothers; always pay when you owe, though not necessarily in money; never be afraid' — a Gypsy saying.

In the crypt of the church of Notre Dame de la Mer, a child and his mother light a candle in honor of the Gypsy saint Sara who served the Marys.

news came to the Bishop of Paris who went there and took with him a Friar of the Minors named Little Jacobin, who by command of the Bishop made a fine preaching, excommunicating all those who had believed them and shown their hands. And they were obliged to depart'. In that last short sentence lies all the history, tragedy and success of the Gypsies.

The first Gypsies fascinated the people they met with their strange language and physical appearance, their skill as beggars and thieves, and their ability to foretell the future. But it was a fascination compounded of fear. This duly gave way to hostility on the part of authority and they were obliged to depart. Until recently this pattern has been continuous in the western world.

No race, except perhaps that of the Jew, is so widely distributed over the face of the earth as the Gypsy. No matter where you travel in Europe, there you will find Gypsies. They are as one would expect, plentiful and widespread in North America. They are in South America, in North Africa, throughout Asia Minor, and eastwards through Persia to the Bay of Bengal. They are in Australia and New Zealand. They have been recorded, though not in recent years, in China and in South Africa.

No race, other than the Jordanian Bedouin nomads who live in desert areas around traditional Bedouin strongholds of the rose-red city of Petra and the Jewish, has been so consistently persecuted. The Nazis exterminated half a million Gypsies. Inevitably, persecution has made the Gypsies suspicious of other Europeans, and perhaps explains the persistence of the characteristics and language they still have in common.

After centuries in Europe the Gypsy way of life has for some time been accepted as a richly colorful part of the rural scene. But the Gypsy himself has been regarded throughout with deep suspicion. The age-old conviction that all Gypsies are liars and thieves remains strong to this day. And the Gypsy certainly did not lose his distrust of the 'gorgio', the non-Gypsy. For many generations his horses and waggons were accepted on the roads. He could tramp by the roadside and not be immediately moved on by the authorities. Those were the golden days.

He could exercise his traditional skill in horse-trading, which was based on a real knowledge of horses and horse medicine. He could practise the traditional Gypsy crafts: as tinsmith (tinker), coppersmith, china mender, basket weaver, maker of clothes pegs. He could do casual work for farmers; blackcurrant-picking, potato-lifting, or harvesting the hops; and he would be welcomed as good and cheap labor. And the goods that the Gypsy woman sold, and her traditional skill of fortune-telling would be equally appreciated.

Now throughout the industrialized western world the Gypsy's golden age is over. It is easy to find reasons. The motor car has eliminated the horse as transport, and so killed the Gypsy horse trade. As modern main roads are much too dangerous for a horse and waggon, the Gypsy has been forced to take to the lorry, or if he's more affluent to car and caravan. This has altered the whole tempo of the Gypsy's life; with a profound effect.

After paying homage to their
saint, Gypsy pilgrims
perform an impromptu concert
of improvised guitar music,
song and dance.

Traditionally a Gypsy meal consisted of a thick soup or stew — today money can buy foods once eaten only by the *gadjé* (non-Gypsy).

Urbanization has spread and reduced the amount of open land available to Gypsies for the camping sites near towns which were of particular value to the nomad. Many of the traditional *atching tans* have disappeared beneath bricks and mortar. Landlords with their eye on future building development now don't allow Gypsies to camp on suitable sites, for which they would be willing and eager to pay rent. Permission tends especially to be refused to the Gypsy with a car and caravan.

Mass production has dealt the Gypsy a further blow. It is killing the Gypsy crafts. Agricultural mechanization, too, has played its part. There is no longer the same demand for seasonal Gypsy labor on the farms. Hops, for example, are now machine-harvested.

But more deadly than all these things is the anti-nomadic social climate. This is the child of bureaucracy, which by definition is hostile to non-conformity. In the Soviet Union Gypsy nomadism was legally ended in 1956; but then the Soviet Union always recognised the Gypsies as a separate race and formal effort has been made to maintain their racial identity. There is a Gypsy Theater in Moscow, their language is officially en-

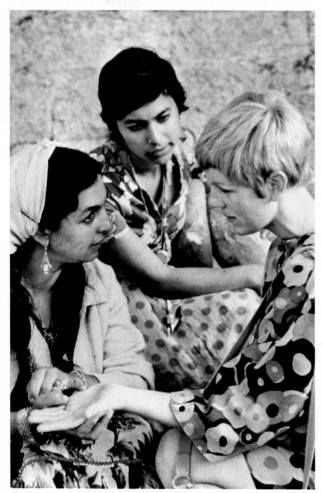

A 15th century chronicler wrote of the Gypsies: 'There were witches who looked into people's hands and told what had happened to them . . .'

For centuries Gypsies have earned a living by fortune telling; 'by magic or by skill they emptied people's pockets and put into theirs.'

Some Gypsies resemble their Indian forebears — but it is their way of life, peddling, trading and farm-laboring, that is most distinctive.

The Gypsy fêtes and fairs are welcomed as a colorful part of rural life. Here a Gypsy performer prepares to 'eat fire.'

couraged, and so on. Much the same has happened in Spain and the Balkans. In Britain, where nomadism is not illegal, the Gypsy has never been recognized officially as a race, but rather regarded as a peculiar type of vagrant. And so no attempt has been made to maintain his racial identity.

The Gypsy, so long tenacious of his nomadic way of life and his Gypsy identity, is now often deprived by circumstance of almost all his traditional ways of earning a living. He is faced with a choice. He can either conform, by adapting to the conditions he finds around him, settling in a house if he can find one, or, failing this, relying on public assistance; or he can continue to be nomadic until authority catches up with him and he is forced off the road.

European Gypsies who meet in the Camargue do not yet conform. They gather for their yearly festivals. But their pilgrimage seems a wish to revive the myth of the Gypsy as a handsome, proud and free man; a myth which substitutes a romantic image for that of a 'noble savage'. In the face of governments who seek to disband them, the Gypsies are no longer truly able to live, as they once did, on the margin of civilization.

Alpine farmers
Evolène village

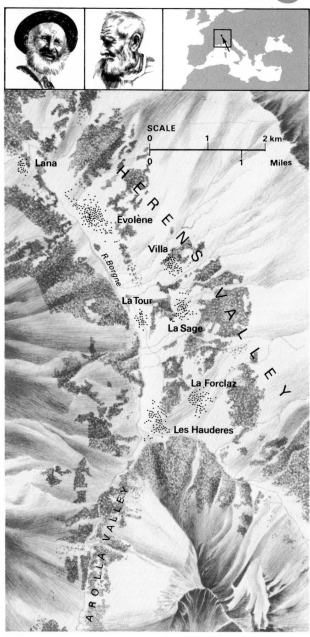

The Alps, the backbone of Europe, sweep in a wide
continuous arc from the Côte d'Azur in the west,
north through France, Italy and Switzerland, then
swing east along the Danube basin through Austria and
finally curve south into Yugoslavia.

Between the major mountain blocks, the main river
valleys form narrow corridors from which wide valleys
branch off into high massifs. Where the lower slopes are
not cultivated they are forested up to about 7,000 feet.
For another thousand feet above the timber line lie the
natural pastures – the *alps* or *alpages* – where livestock
graze in summer. Beyond them are the ice and rock of

As the winter snows melt in
April sheep are driven to
graze around the village. In
summer they will roam the
high *alpages*.

the mountain peaks.

Throughout the Alps the snow means that farms can only be worked in summer. Most of the annual precipitation falls as snow. The winters are long and cold, the summers short and dry, and the agricultural cycle has to be compressed into the summer months. During the relatively idle winter months, when livestock is kept inside and there is deep snow on the fields, the mountain farmers have to find other sources of income. In the past these were usually a combination of local crafts – wood carving, watchmaking or weaving – and temporary migration to the lowland towns or farming areas in search of work.

Today there are new economic opportunities: tourism, based on the scenery and recreations of the mountains; heavy industry, based on the hydro-electric power; light industry, developed from the craft heritage. These opportunities have been encouraged by governments as agriculture has declined in importance. As communications have opened up the mountain areas, the mountain people have had contact with lowland towns and begun to look for a better standard of living which they could never have achieved through farming alone. They have also found themselves brought into a fiercely competitive market economy in which they find it increasingly difficult to hold their own. The margin between viability and non-viability on their farms has always been small. Now it is more important than ever for them to find subsidiary or alternative sources of income. The alpine communities are continually having to adapt to a modern world.

The typical alpine community is a large central village and a number of hamlets. The farmers live in little homesteads clustered together and surrounded by a patchwork of small fields, often divided by narrow irrigation ditches. Their houses are large and many-storied, for they were built not only as living areas but as agricultural complexes. Stables and storage cellars are on the ground floor, often cut into the slope of the mountain. Living space is on the first floor, and the upper storeys, which are often open at the gable ends, are barns for drying and storing hay. In most alpine villages the old, open gable houses contrast with the newly built or converted flats, hotels, bars and tourist shops; there are villagers dressed in traditional costume and others in snappy modern clothes; there are people who speak the old local language or patois and others who speak the national language. These contrasts reflect social and economic change, but they also reflect the resistance of the traditional peasant system to change, much as they have resisted their harsh and unfavorable environment.

Many alpine farmers farm in the traditional family way. For them agriculture is not an industry like modern farming in which one farmer, or a group of farmers, competes to maximize production and sell produce on the market at the highest possible price. For these farmers agriculture is unlikely to produce wealth. It is not even a job. It is a way of life in which the family labors on the family land to ensure not profit, but secure survival. There is no sense of competition among farmers. They constantly help each other out.

The number of stock a family owns depends on the number they can maintain. It depends on the land they own and the labor they can muster. In summer when sheep and cattle graze on the communally-owned high pastures the farmer and his family must grow and harvest enough fodder in their own fields to keep their stock throughout the winter, when the animals are brought down from the pastures and stalled in the homesteads. The yield of the land will in turn depend on the number of their stock; for manure, accumulated in winter, is used to fertilize the fields. Land and labor also affect the kind of stock the family can raise. The communally-owned grazing land may be steep and rocky and better suited to sheep which need relatively little attention. Or it may be lush grass and better for cows, which need more constant care than sheep; and the transport and processing of milk is time-consuming.

The peasant-farmer's fields are small, widely scattered across the community's territory and quite unsuitable for modern farming methods. His attachment to his land, so often represented as a sentimental tie, is in fact based on the most intimate knowledge of his fields so that he can take every possible advantage of variations in altitude, aspect, steepness, soil depth and quality. He must have the utmost expertise in planning his crops for some will inevitably fail in the frequent natural disasters of the mountains – sudden frosts, droughts and floods – and he must in advance offset their loss. So he plans ahead, not in anticipation of future market trends, but in the expectation of calamities with which he is familiar.

In the Alps the family is the traditional basic unit of society, whether the immediate one of parents and children or the extended one which includes cousins and more distant relatives. Where there are still subsistence farmers, it is also a family enterprise, of which the farmer is director and his son both employee and director-elect. The family is its own labor force and not only produces but also consumes its own crops, which never reach any external market. Labor, in a system like this, cannot be costed in market terms: the produce, like the labor, stays in the family. Economic incentives of making money and achieving a high standard of living matter less than family independence, a high reputation with the neighbors, and bringing up children.

Each family household needs help from outside the family at the busiest times in the agricultural year, so family independence does not mean family self-sufficiency. So precarious is the existence of every family that it must give and receive help from other farming households: the separate farms are economically interdependent.

The village 'judge' (mayor) samples wines and cheese kept in the *cave* adjoining the animal stalls that form the ground floor of his home.

(Bottom) Valleyhead Swiss communities like Evolène, Herens Valley, live traditionally several thousand feet up in the ridged Alps.

Breeding fighting cows (not bulls), matched in bouts of strength at the *'combat des reines'* festival is a major activity among Valais folk.

The farming families were linked by kinship, and kinship is still a justification for giving and receiving help. Father, mother and children – the basic kin unit – now share the freehold rights in land and property. When primogeniture used to prevail younger sons either emigrated or remained single so that they could preserve the family holding intact.

Unlike the outsiders who have moved into the mountains the villagers are united by strong ties of kinship, economic interdependence, a common culture and a sense of community identity. And these values have also operated at a higher level of political organization. These communities demonstrated political independence by organizing themselves into semi-autonomous Cantons and Federal Republics. And then there was their tendency to participate in the separatist religious movements such as the 12th century Vaudois movement in France and later in the Protestant Reformation movements such as Calvinism and Zwingliism.

Although remote and isolated, the alpine regions were nevertheless crossed and contained by international frontiers, and were of great strategic importance. At various times Catholic neighbors, abetted by the Vatican, cut trans-alpine trade which would have benefited popular Protestant movements in Austria, Germany, Czechoslovakia and even Switzerland itself. And the 57 self-sufficient alpine communities were drawn, sometimes forcibly into national affairs. In this sense there has never been a separate alpine rural society. Like all peasantries the alpine farmers belonged politically and economically to the nations of which they were a part.

This has never been more true than today when all the alpine nations must solve their common problem of agricultural decline. The development policies of the French, Swiss, Italian, Austrian and Yugoslavian governments to improve and finance agriculture, tourism and industrial development vary not only from country to country but from 'planning region' to 'planning region.' The solutions vary. But the problems are almost exactly the same. They are based on the common factors of ecology, historical development and the special social structure of the tiny alpine communities.

These are communities in which everybody knows, and keeps bumping into, everybody else. And a man's reputation among his fellow villagers is very important. In these fiercely egalitarian alpine communities prestige depends not on income or occupation, which vary so little, but on a man's performance as husband, father, farmer, craftsman and villager.

Today the peasant must participate in the market economy if he is to maintain the security, reputation and continuity of his family. He must overcome his traditional belief that economic incentives are subordinate to family well-being. The peasant must become a modern farmer; the shrewd entrepreneur who makes the right, price-conscious, economic decisions or else pays the price of failure. In some areas agriculture has been reorganized so that it provides a reasonable income and standard of living. But in many more areas a market orientation has meant that agriculture has had to be abandoned as a primary means of production and livelihood. The change is gradual for as new jobs are taken up, men continue to work the land to ensure diversity of income. For many, the decline of agriculture has meant permanent emigration to the lowlands. During the first half of this century many of the alpine areas became seriously depopulated.

Although the development of industry keeps many farmers busy in winter it is the recent growth of tourism which has come with the popularity of camping, climbing and skiing which is most helpful. Skiing provides employment during the winter and turns to advantage the previous disadvantage of heavy snowfall. Tourism enables many to participate in the new economy as it provides a variety of tasks for the villagers. They let rooms, act as ski instructors and guides, and keep hotels or shops. Tourism puts a speculative value on land for building which is detrimental to agricultural re-organization. For those brought up to see the land's cultivation as the family's livelihood the sale of land often involves highly upsetting decisions. It undermines a familiar and honored way of life; on the other hand it provides the

Melting Matterhorn snows provide constant summer water for Val d'Heren, as other glaciered peaks do for many similar alpine communities.

(Right) Cattle winter for six months – in *écuries* beneath their owners' homes – on fodder humped down in summer by men and mules.

initial capital for peasant families to enter commerce. And the building industry is another important source of employment for villagers.

Socially the villages are greatly affected by economic change. Outsider families come and live in the communities. Villagers increasingly marry outsiders and so now all members of the village are no longer related. New occupations lessen the dependence of families on each other and increase income differences. So the village communities have become less egalitarian. Yet traditional occupations and values flourish alongside the new jobs and aspirations to new standards of living. The peasant who unloads manure from a mule in the fields may be the owner of a new bar. The old man in his working clothes, conspicuous among the smart tourists, may own the most desirable building site in the village. Many retired people continue to work the land and look after livestock when there is no economic need. There are still preferences for home-grown vegetables – even though supermarket prices are cheaper – and for cooking on wood – though houses may have oil-fired central heating. These are the remaining symbols of a way of life based on traditional values. Adhering to them still confers a certain prestige among villagers.

Traditional values not only survive; they often determine the direction of change. The ideal of the family enterprise remains: the villagers who have the greatest commercial success are those whose children participate in the business. Local entrepreneurs still depend on their reputation with other villagers, because their social life still centers on the village community and their commercial success depends so often on the villagers' cooperation over such matters as new development and planning proposals.

The scale and type of development depends ultimately on the extent of government or private investment. Many problems arise out of the differences between the aims of the large-scale developer and the values of a small-scale society. The alpine peasant has always been ready to adapt to changing conditions and opportunities in accordance with his particular view of the world.

(Far right) Cut off from the outside influences in steep-sided, isolated valleyheads many southern alpine women prefer the old dress and ways.

(Right) Evolène folk keep up their spinning and their *patois*. 450,000 people in Grisons valley talk crude Latin – Romansch.

The people of southern Italy

Hardy fishermen daily brave
the Straits of Messina where
once the mythical treacherous
sirens, Scylla and Charybdis,
lured sailors onto the rocks.

In the southernmost part of mainland Italy are the three regions of Puglia, Basilicata (also known as Lucania) and Calabria. In the boot-shape of Italy on the map rugged, mountainous Calabria to the south-west is the toe; Basilicata is the sole; and at the south-eastern extremity Puglia – with its low-lying plains looking across the sea towards North Africa and the Middle East – is the heel.

If you go from the wealthy and powerful centers of Italy – Rome, Naples, Milan – and travel down into the interior of southern Italy, the change is drastic. Southern Italy seems quite a different country. It is uniquely in- 61 hospitable. There are fat olive trees which men love to sit under when the sun is high. But the soil is rough and the colors stark and dry. To dig is a backbreaking labor with scant reward. And there is much disease. In the 19th century more people died there of malaria than in all other regions of Italy put together. Even middle-aged men remember farm laborers dying by the roadside on their way back from the fields to the towns, which were built on hilltops less congenial – as science was to discover – to the malarial mosquito.

Even at the end of day, a traveler from western Europe would be oppressed by the ceaseless white glare of the houses and the ever-present hazy shimmer of heat that blurs everything in sight. The southern Italians are themselves affected by the unchanging harshness of their lives and land.

In the Calabrian town of Costenza, a huge peasant

Retired peasants are entitled to old-age pensions but only get them if they have backed the party that won the last election.

with baggy trousers, smock and beret, rides in on his donkey every evening. His swinging feet almost touch the ground but the passive face, brown as a polished walnut and heavy with the solemnity of a general entering a defeated town, expresses no humor. A few youths with flashy wristwatches and shiny black pointed shoes shout a barely respectful good evening. Meanwhile slender girls link arms with bell-shaped mothers and set off for the evening promenade. Their snooty air will be short-lived, for soon they get married and in an astonishingly short time their figures rival their mothers' for size. Many of the disgruntled youths settle down, but 'America' – spoken with baited breath – crops up again and again in conversation. Many despair of the dusty sameness of the town-life, the meanness of the rock-strewn soil and their parents' stubborn clinging to old ways. They make off to the big cities or even cross the Atlantic.

They have been drawn away to Rome, Turin, Milan. Between 1870 and World War I thousands poured into the Americas and Australia. After 1950 they swelled the populaces of Switzerland, Belgium, Germany and France. Five million southern Italians have left since the last century, and many more have gone to work for short periods elsewhere.

Southern Italy has over the ages absorbed influences from other parts of the Mediterranean. When Aeneas left Carthage he made his landfall at Cape Palinuro. Words in some of the dialects are borrowed from Arabic. Metaponto (the name is Greek) has the ruins of a Temple of Pythagoras. Taranto has a fine museum of Greek antiquities. There are nine towns in Salento and four in Calabria where the dialect is Greek. Albanian is spoken in some Calabrian villages. The great yearly trade fair at Bari is called the Fair of the Levant. Bari and Brindisi have petrol refineries because they are so convenient for the Middle East oilfields.

Agriculture is the main occupation: wheat and olives are the chief products but the Agrarian Reform of 1951 has encouraged southerners to grow grapes, peaches, tomatoes, artichokes, lemons, mandarins and oranges as well. The plains of Puglia and Metaponto, once winter pastures for mountain sheep and cattle, are more and more prosperous. Fishing gives some people a living, but makes a negligible contribution to the economy. About four per cent of the population now work in industry: in traditional small local industries, and in heavy industry recently set up by the government.

It is hard to get a pension, government aid, or a job. According to Roman Law a bureaucrat must try to keep the state's money from the grasping hands of the citizens. Anglo-Saxons, accustomed to the idea that a civil service exists for the common good of the citizens, are often shocked by the obstacles which the Italian state puts in the ways of its citizens. South Italians expect to extract their rights with difficulty – paying fees, using

The mushroom-topped church of the Calabrian village of Stilo was built 1,200 years ago in the style of Byzantium (now Istanbul).

The people of southern Italy

influence, passing bribes.

They have a number of political options. They may insist on their rights as citizens; pull strings through friends and relations; or rely on community or class solidarity. Insisting on your rights only works in minor matters such as an application for accurate certificates of tax liability or of family status or for a passport. In some towns even routine matters require the personal approach: a patient who wants a medical certificate brings letters of recommendation from the priest to the doctor; a local politician or landowner recommends his elector or employee to the head nurse in the out-patients' clinic, and so on.

Any application which affects the state's resources requires subtle, sometimes serpentine, manoeuvres partly because the resources are limited. Pensions for peasant farmers, for example, are recent innovations and there are more people entitled to them than there are funds; state aid for agricultural improvement is likewise too small to turn a backward area overnight into an up-to-

Puglians have for centuries built *trulli*: unaccountably beehive-shaped houses. A gilt replica is top prize at the Albarobello Pop Festival.

South Italy is notoriously hot, yet this woman wears two underskirts on the theory that the more you wear, the better you keep the heat out.

date paradise. Whether a road is built in one area or another; whether an old peasant gets his pension or has to wait on the list; all depends on personal influence wielded through friendship, kinship or clientship.

The wealthy are the people who wield the influence. They can talk man-to-man with high officials in the provincial capitals; they can give orders to clerks in the town council offices. So poorer people attach themselves to wealthier people. As fortunes have risen and fallen quickly in some towns since the turn of the century wealthy men tend to have poor kinsmen. A poor man can invite a rich man to be his child's godfather or sponsor at a wedding. The poor seek every means to seal bonds with men of influence – employees with the boss; tenants with the landowner; craftsmen with important clients; husbands of devout members of Catholic Action with priests.

But today political parties have replaced the wealthy as patrons of the poor. They secure or promise government aid for the community in return for their votes. On behalf of their members they approach state agencies, help with getting pensions and so on. Politics are patronage, a question of having the right friends, cultivating the right relations or being a good boss or client. The difference between government patronage and the older patron-client system is that it is a straight exchange of votes against benefits. This has disadvantages.

The people of southern Italy

The men shake the olive trees and the women pick up the olives. A woman who works for wages for her neighbors loses prestige.

This man had ten brothers; only he remained in rugged Calabria. The rest emigrated — three to Australia, the others to the USA.

Inheritance is complex and often leads to quarrels between families. The men say it is the women whose gossip stirs up the trouble.

Almost all southern Italians live in cramped towns perched on hilltops less accessible to the mosquito that brings malaria.

Now the promise of a job is understood to be conditional on 'proper voting.' Political affairs – elections, petitions to ministers, the delicate art of coalition-making – involve the distribution of much-needed state resources. In one town in Lucania the government's contribution to the Poor Relief fund dried up when a minister's portrait was removed from the council chamber. Allegiances to political parties are based not on class identity or on ideology, but on hope of reward.

As poor men compete for benefits from magnates allegiances cover the whole of society, uniting people of different rank. Solidarity between people of similar rank and wealth is rare. Nevertheless collective interests do occasionally find expression, especially where property is distributed in so many small lots that most landowners have too little land. Economic depression sometimes results in collective action. In the late 19th century, before and after World War I and after World War II, there were labor riots, estates were taken over and

co-operatives were set up. But these class movements quickly die down.

Only on rare occasions are the provinces politically united. Recently they have engaged in fierce argument over the site of the new regional headquarters. Sometimes the populace of a town will draw together when its collective pride is injured. But the region remains a network of isolated communities which have developed their own peculiar ways of coming to terms with life.

In the mountains there is no industry; agriculture is miserable. When the great forests of the interior were cut down, the exposed topsoil was soon eroded, and the climate, which was moderately humid because of the trees, deteriorated.

Almost everyone in southern Italy lives in towns strikingly placed on hilltops. The further the towns are to the east the larger they are likely to be, and the nearer to sea-level: they vary in population from about two to twenty-five thousand. Large conglomerations of people tend to accumulate in one rather inaccessible town for no apparent historical reason. But agriculture is poor and undemanding: wheat and olives require little attention and do not give much of a living. It is convenient to live in an urban center where opportunities for casual work can be seized at short notice.

A man's reputation depends to a large extent on the women for whom he is responsible. They too must live in towns where they can be kept under the constant surveillance of neighbors and relations who can publicize their excellence. Men have two tasks: keeping an eye on the girls and supporting the wife. They are expected to control their women. As fathers and brothers they must ensure that the girls in their care are chaste and modest. As husbands they must provide their wives with food, fuel and clothes. Wives are expected to be faithful. Husbands are expected to work hard and prosper. Behavior like fighting or keeping a mistress, gambling or drinking to excess, which deprive the family of food is bad. A disreputable man is the man who has failed as a provider or as a defender of the chastity of his women. His two duties are closely associated. Women who work in the country often have husbands too poor to support them: they work 'to feed the family': this is also a charitable explanation for a poor woman's adultery with a social superior, such as an employer or priest.

There is much social change because parents fall prey to stupid ambitions for their children. The shoemaker wants his son to become an accountant; the sausage vendor wants his son to become a physician. Just imagine such foolishness – says an official primary school book of the 1950s. Above all, parents want to see their children well-married. As old-fashioned peasant agriculture becomes increasingly inadequate, they are often anxious that their children should not work the land – although they are often discouraged from bettering their children's status. Most peasant children would rather be building laborers 67

Wheat and olive growing usually pays best. But there is always a good catch for night fishermen of the volcano isle of Stromboli.

In southern Italy women help the men even with manual labor. Few can afford to be lazy. Over 5 million people have emigrated this century.

These women of Albanian descent in traditional dress talk in front of a chicken-hut. 'Lost' chickens cause many a quarrel.

or factory workers than work the land.

Social advancement requires education: degrees in commerce from the university at Bari and across the straits at Messina can be won merely by attending the examination. In poor families the elder brothers and sisters often work with their father to pay for a good education for the youngest who is expected eventually to return to the village to ply his profession: the glory extends to his family, who may also gain materially. There is a great surplus not only of the traditional lawyers but now also of teachers.

In the past the priesthood was the most popular profession. A powerful but unmarriageable (if not celibate) brother could be expected to devote most of his influence to furthering his brothers' and sisters' interests. True, he might have bastards (or mules, as they are sometimes called) and he would look after them. But mules are mules, and legitimate brothers and sisters and their children take precedence. Other professions are now more lucrative, and perhaps more powerful.

Property is inherited in all sorts of ways. In one town parents give sons a house and daughters a trousseau at marriage; land is divided among them when the parents die. In the next town, property may be handed on when the children marry: daughters get houses, a trousseau and land; sons get land. Customs chop and change from town to town. The consequences may be significant. A marriage of a man from a town where daughters get houses, to a woman from a town where sons get them, requires such delicate negotiations that they actually deter such matches. The problem of parents who are obliged to make property arrangements which flout the conventions is to maintain their prestige and reputation as good parents.

Parents who control all their property till they die often earn their children's contempt. Parents who hand over their property at their children's marriages are usually allowed a peaceful and respected old age. But then there are often frequent angry quarrels between brothers.

As the children do not all marry at once property may be divided over twenty years. During this time property may improve; values may go up. Parents who improve their remaining land by planting vines or olives, or digging a well, can make a son who has already got his share unimproved feel aggrieved. Whether the parents are dead or alive division of property is always tricky. Successive divisions, as the children marry, breed quarrels. Wives and their families are blamed for stirring up the innate greed of the men and sowing dissension between brothers. It is not surprising that priests, who have no wives, are a favorite sort of brother.

The entire system may change if the south becomes widely industrialized; but complicated customs of inheritance do not immediately disappear when the economy changes. If industrial workers behaved quite differently from peasants, they could only marry among themselves. Land may become less valuable, but people still want it as it gives security, yields food and has symbolic worth. It is better to own land, even of little value, than to own nothing and be a *nullatenente*.

69

The Parisians
France

70

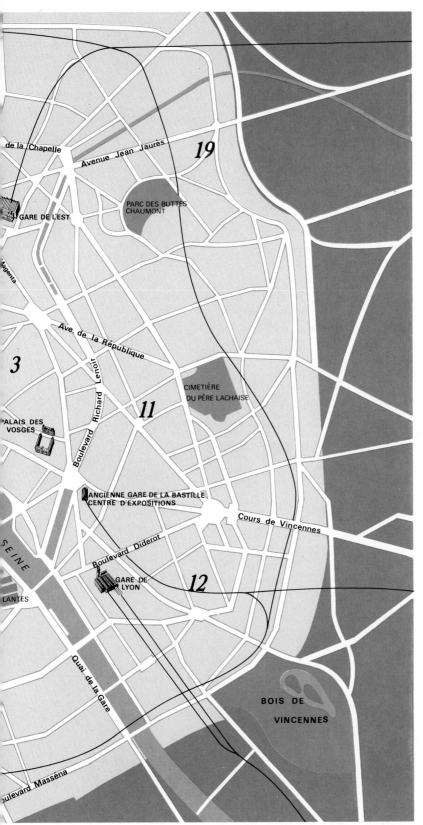

Baron Haussmann gave Frenchmen the world's most beautiful capital. Medieval Paris comprised districts 1-7. The deep purple area is suburbs.

Like many European cities, Paris has undergone profound environmental and social changes since the war. The once so magnetic and magical city – hymned in a thousand dreamy cabaret songs – has become a sprawling megalopolis, ill-equipped with public services and ill-organized. The Parisians' prosperity and housing have improved, but at the cost of some of the old charm of their city. Its population has swollen since 1945 from six to nine million, while London's in the same period has actually fallen. More than two Parisians in three now live in suburbia, in anonymous new high-rise blocks; less than one third (2·6 million) are true 'Parisians' who still inhabit the 'Ville de Paris' within the old city gates. This is the historic Paris that the tourist sees, of lovers under the chestnut-trees or *sous-les-ponts-de-Paris,* of little bistros and *la douceur de vivre.*

Parisians are the first to admit that their city has lost some of its old identity. Behind this change there are three factors. First, the cultural malaise. Paris ceased some twenty years ago to be the world's cultural capital, unrivaled generator of art and ideas; and today even the notoriously ostrich-like left-bank intelligentsia have finally got round to accepting the unpleasant possibility that creatively they are second-rate. Are not most of the good new plays in Paris foreign imports? The causes of this cultural decline are hard to define: most probably it is that the post-war French have become so pre-occupied

71

Haussmann became Prefect of Paris after the riots of 1848. His fine boulevards radiating from the Arc de Triomphe gave troops a line of fire.

with technology, industrial growth, and the values of a get-rich-quick society that, relatively, they have lost interest in the arts. Whereas many brilliant young British people seek careers in the artistic world, especially the BBC, their French counterparts prefer to go into industry or the higher civil service.

A second factor is political. Paris much more than the provinces bore the brunt of the humiliations and upheavals of the period from 1940 to 1962, from the Nazi parades on the Champs-Elysées to the last sickening months of the Algerian crisis when there were terrorist bomb attacks and police raids all over the city. Older people are still scarred by the Occupation period, when Frenchmen lived in fear of reprisals or denunciation as much from each other as from the enemy and many were corrupted by the black market. This partly explains their tenseness and lack of fellow-feeling today. More recently the 1968 student explosions have created new tensions. Even today, despite the wealth and stability under Pompidou, the sight of grim-faced riot police in the Latin Quarter is a constant reminder to Parisians that they are not at ease with themselves.

The third factor is practical and the most important. Parisians today are paying the price of nearly a century of neglect of town planning. In the Ville de Paris they still live more densely than in any other major capital, including Manhattan or Tokyo. They live 106 to the acre, against 43 in London. They have less than half the green park space, per head, of a New Yorker or a Londoner. Since the war they have allowed the rapid increase of personal prosperity, business activity and population, to outstrip the growth of public services such as hospitals – and many private ones such as taxis and plumbing. Public transport is especially inadequate, and this simply gives the individualistic Parisian an added reason to use his own car. So the old *douceur de vivre* is blotted out by the fumes, noise and traffic-jams. On the picturesque left bank big cars slither up to park on the pavements of alleys meant for hand-carts.

Parisians created these problems, but they are temperamentally ill-suited to cope with them. A more civic-minded people might have more success in grouping together to find remedies or put pressure on the authorities. A more placid people might put up with the daily irritations more calmly. But, restless and self-willed, they find their nerves stretched taut – they are late for appointments, snappy on the telephone, and can barely stem their indignation when the plumber will not come. Life is much more pleasant today in the provinces which were once thought so dull. And some Parisians are finally coming to realise it. Some are even migrating to work there, especially to pleasant and prosperous southern towns like Grenoble and Toulouse.

Like most Frenchmen, Parisians are conservative people who have recently discovered a passion for modernism. While eager to adapt to a new material

72

Military ceremonies were encouraged under de Gaulle but lately Parisians, notably the young, have seemed less interested in *la gloire*.

Paris' history of rioting is varied and ancient. Louis XVI might have survived 1789 (the Revolution) with today's police and their CS gas.

Students rather than the masses form the bulk of the present generation of Paris' street demonstrators. Riot police are fearsome.

Douceur de vivre is not entirely eliminated by fumes, noise and traffic jams. There are still the chestnut trees and young love beneath them.

world of glamor, gadgets and technical efficiency, they cling for security to old habits, rituals and social attitudes. In fact they are wary of altering the inner fabric of their lives and of society. This conflict lies at the root of nearly every aspect of modern Parisian life and leads to some strange anomalies. A firm may invest in costly new computers and other devices and yet fail to eliminate the inhibiting hierarchy and formal routines of French work-relationships, which limit the usefulness of the new hardware. Everyone wants fast cars and seaside holidays, yet clings to the tradition of going away only in high summer: thus the roads and resorts are jammed and the hotels put out of business for most of the year.

These are just two examples. The rigid constraints of tradition are clearly reflected in the Parisian class 73

The Parisians France

The Folies Bergère has lost its monopoly of fashionable wickedness but not its world reputation for inimitably Parisian professionalism.

Artist from Monmartre, retired restaurateur and priest who has heard a generation's confessions belong to Paris, and Paris to them.

To film director René Clair *(Sous les toits de Paris)* rooftop Paris meant youth, love and poverty. Impecunious old occupy the cramped attics, too.

Bohemia and the bourgeoisie tend to keep their distance. Only a conspicuously successful artist is likely to be taken up by 'society.'

structure. Today the working-class with its new prosperity emulates the bourgeois life-style, while remaining severely separate. There has been less post-war social revolution than in London. The French, though possibly less class-conscious than the British, are still divided by class: their classes do not mix. They depersonalize their conflicts, taking political pot-shots at one another from behind sheltering barricades. Class divisions are not a matter of financial status, as in the United States, for many skilled workers today earn more than the genteel lower-middle *rentier* class, whose savings are eroded by inflation. Political tradition and, as in Britain, education are largely to blame. The State *lycées* (high schools) are in theory free and open to all, but in practice they are still very much a middle-class preserve, especially the famous ones in central Paris. As universities accept only candidates from the *lycées*, many able young people from working homes rarely get the chance of a higher education. There are no formal boundaries, but often timidity or a kind of inverted pride keeps workers out of the *lycées*. Whatever the reasons, this class still feels in some way 'alienated' from French life, and so plows its grievances into voting Communist. All this is beginning to change, but slowly.

Within each class, Parisian society is more compartmented than, for example, London society. A series of little cliques tend to ignore each other, or are mutually suspicious. The socialite world of *le tout-Paris* is one class. Here are found the few thousand celebrities and millionaires who attend the society balls and put on their glad-rags for the races at Longchamps or the Opéra galas. In this milieu, the professions do mix – a film star, a tycoon and a champion boxer may well hobnob together. But below this thin upper crust, the professional worlds divide. Bohemia is less acceptable to the rest of the bourgeoisie than to middle-class Londoners. Parties where a Marxist professor chats up a debby model, or a stiff-suited banker is in earnest discussion with a scruffy-jerseyed sculptor are rare. Bankers stay with bankers, bohemians with bohemians. Parisians take their political differences rather less in the spirit of a club than 75

Upper crust

One of the strangest of these enclosed worlds is the aristocracy. Once it set a tone in France and all Europe for taste, gallantry and prowess. Now it has been pushed onto the sidelines of national life, tolerated but ignored. Gossip-columnists ignore its divorces and other scandals because the public is not interested. Because there is no French monarchy to provide a titular leadership, the aristocracy has lost its *raison-d'etre* and its prestige. Yet it keeps its pride. Aristocrats, when they are not involved in keeping their costly provincial *châteaux*, cling together in Paris in their small but exclusive world. They invite each other to formal cocktail parties or an occasional ball or banquet with echoes of past glories. Many are cultured, gentle, liberal people, less acquisitive than the bourgeoisie.

The bourgeoisie is still the backbone of the nation and of Paris. Some bourgeois families live in old-fashioned flats in the central part of Paris. They are usually furnished in classical style: elegant but severe, with rarely a relaxing sofa, just spindly straight-backed chairs. Increasingly however, more of the bourgeoisie are buying comfortable modern flats in the newer suburbs: families gravitate towards plush new housing estates that emulate Californian-style glamor, complete with sun-terraces and built-in barbecues, with names like 'la Résidence

Dinner party *moeurs* tend to be rigidly observed – with printed invitations, evening dress, and gloved footmen (sometimes hired).

Upper class Parisian children have little chance to get dirty or run wild. Manners are good, and private school standards are high.

Paris' social élite contains an aristocratic remnant whose opulent life-style is nowadays based on success in business rather than large estates.

The elegant Second Empire houses of the 16th *arrondissement* (district) with their high ceilings and grand stairways now have good plumbing too.

If girls are to get by in Parisian high society they must know how to cut a pear without getting sticky fingers. Hence the instruction.

Upper crust

Elysée.'

The life-style of the bourgeois Parisian is changing. But old customs die hard. He is becoming a commuter. Yet he still sets off to work with little more in his belly than a *croissant* or bun washed down with strong coffee. *Le breakfast anglais* is more admired than consumed. Only reluctantly, under the pressure of big-city growth, does the Parisian give up the cherished tradition of returning home each day for the ritual of a two-hour family lunch. Most who live centrally still do; so do some commuters, even though it means taking four painful journeys a day. But other commuters have given up the unequal struggle. To accommodate them, firms have begun to cut their lunch-break from two hours to one. Here again is an example of the way traditions in France are in conflict with economic change. Only in the past few years have shops and banks in central Paris started to remain open from 12 to 2 pm. In the provinces where lunch is still sacred, they close.

The Parisian works frenetically hard, often staying in his office till 7.30 pm or 8 pm. Much of this time is lost in battling with other Frenchmen, who are disinclined to

The social 'Season' in Paris retains a flavor of Edwardian elegance — racing at Longchamps, gala balls for charity, and — as here — the Opera.

Upper crust

For the well-to-do, 'le weekend' — for example in St Tropez on the Côte d'Azur — has become a regular element in the pattern of Parisian life.

SEM

Chez "Maxim's"

78

Today's menu of Maxim's recalls that for generations gourmets and aristocrats from all over the world have flocked to Paris for its *haute cuisine*.

The energetically rich hunt stag in style in the forêt de Chantilly — about thirty miles north of the capital.

return telephone calls when asked, or answer letters. He has more nervous energy than most mortals and seems to survive on five or six hours' sleep a night; but after battling his way back from the office in the traffic jams, he is worn out. He may then relax over an apéritif in one of the many sidewalk cafés. But the café habit is declining. Now the cafés on the Champs-Elysées seem mostly frequented by foreigners.

When the Parisian gets home he is not very sociable. After coping with work and Paris, he and his wife want to hug their privacy to themselves, or share it with a few close friends and family. This partly accounts for the French reputation for inhospitality, which in fact applies only to Paris. Provincials are as hospitable as in most countries. Parisians lack time, but they are also inhibited by their traditions of elegant formality. Most families want either to entertain in style or not at all – and style, in the upper bourgeoisie, often means elaborately-laid tables and servants in uniform. 'I can't have anyone to dinner this month' a leisured housewife once said. 'You see, my maid has hurt her leg.' In Parisian 'society,' dinner-party habits are still those of Edwardian London with printed cards, probably evening dress, white-gloved, hired waiters, and rigid conventions about serving the correct food and wines. Drinks parties, except among the very young, tend to be prim little 'cocktails', always

79

In at the kill — a crowd of foot followers. Hunting on horseback is more popular than before World War II. Less wealthy go shooting.

Blue collar worker

For an average working class family with two children state welfare payments amount to about half the husband's wages.

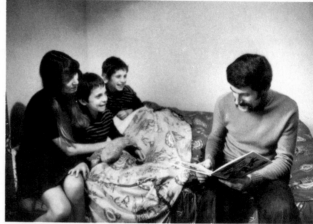

with the same neat *canapés* and conventional talk, a style that has set the tone for diplomatic receptions around the globe. Younger people, it is true, are trying to desert this tradition. They may now give *saucisson-et-vin-rouge* parties where one eats off one's lap. But Parisians are often ill-at-ease with such informality, which rarely suits the furniture or décor of the older flats, and either do not give many parties at all, or extend a casual invitation to supper at a few hours' notice, adding apologetically '*ça sera a la fortune du pot,*' as if ashamed to betray the old ceremonial standards.

The Parisians' social relations tend to be directed towards the family, as in other Latin societies. It is not uncommon to find parties of thirty or forty guests, all of whom are related, although the extended clan-like family is losing importance to the smaller 'nuclear' family of parents and children. This is especially true in the upper bourgeoisie, where earned income is now more important than family property and family managements, which have declined. Young couples today prefer motoring or the privacy of a weekend cottage to the traditional clan reunion, subject of a thousand bitter novels. Although people see less of their cousins and aunts than they used

to, they are still closely tied to the more immediate family. 'I had to cancel my holiday in Greece this summer' a sophisticated young woman teacher said 'Because my grandmother got ill and my mother was worried.' Her English counterpart would rarely display such a sense of duty. Parisians make few close friends, and depend less upon them. They may chat easily to strangers in a train or café, but they tend to be more reserved when it comes to forming real ties. The use of Christian names is still restricted, by British and especially by American standards, though it is growing – especially among the young – and is far more widespread than in Germany. Two men, firm friends in the same job, call each other *tu* but also use surnames, while their wives, though they meet often, go on addressing one another as *Madame* and *vous*.

Nowhere are middle-class habits changing faster than in that most hallowed of French domains, gastronomy. The French still eat far better than any other nation in the west, and still take eating relatively seriously. They talk about it endlessly, comparing the merits of this week's *coq au vin* with last week's in a way that most Anglo-Saxons would find boring. But the wind of change is blowing through bistros and domestic kitchens. The

80

(Top) At least half the working-class families of Paris have been rehoused since the war – mainly in new 'high-rise' suburban blocks.

(Above) Lunch is an important part of the family's day. As often as possible they eat together – and drink a bottle of *vin ordinaire*.

(Above) Parisian workers are better off than ever before. The *appartement* may be cramped – but there's a new cooker and refrigerator.

(Right) Militant Renault car workers: only 25% French workers are unionized, but a major issue can bring out 100,000 to march in Paris.

The old can no longer count on being looked after by their own families. More than 30% now live alone in poverty or else in 'homes.'

Blue collar worker

young middle-class housewife is no longer prepared to spend hours on the servitude of *plats mijotés* as her grandmother did. And her husband no longer expects it. He does not mind if she just pops a steak under the grill. When dining out the younger bourgeoisie go less for the big gastronomic meal in drab surroundings, and more for an 'amusing' atmosphere in restaurants where the food is less good. They will accept formerly despised foreign *cuisines*, such as Greek or Italian. They will even enjoy candlelight, whereas formerly Parisians thought it essential to see what they were eating. Many older people are trying to keep the flag of *haute cuisine* flying – but even they worry increasingly about their livers.

Holidays have assumed a greater importance than *cuisine* now, with the growing pressures of work in Paris. From early July, office workers think of little else, and in August the city is empty. Parisians take longer annual holidays than any other city-dwellers: five weeks for the working-class, an average of six to ten weeks for the middle-class. They now favor holidays abroad, whereas before the war they rarely strayed outside their frontiers. These new needs are satisfied in that unique Parisian middle-class phenomenon, the Club Méditerranée. At the club's summer 'villages,' in Corfu perhaps, or in Sicily, Parisians discard their sophisticated dress in favor of sarongs and bead-necklaces. They sleep in straw huts, call each other *tu*, and indulge in an anonymous sensual camaraderie that contrasts vividly with their rigid, stratified society at home. This fantasy world provides Parisians with an escape back to their peasant origins, a heritage which life in Paris has almost obliterated. Parisians are also becoming very *sportif*; formerly so sedentary, they now drive long distances for winter skiing weekends in the distant Alps. The English word 'weekend' they have taken into their language, and adopted the habit with a special appetite. All over the Ile-de-France and beyond, they have been buying up old farmsteads and villas to refurnish as weekend country cottages.

Despite this new mobility, they are coming to care more than before about their homes, both for the weekend and in town. They are channeling their new prosperity into better homes and furnishing rather than into better food and drink. They now spend almost as great a proportion of their budget on this as Anglo-Saxons. Many people buy graceful but tumble-down old houses in the lovelier parts of Paris, such as the Marais or Ile-St-Louis and restore them elegantly and at great cost, filling them with antique furniture. Others favor the very latest electronic gimmicks in the most modish modern flats. Again this illustrates the competing forces of tradition and novelty.

If the novelties are of Anglo-American origin, they are all the more popular. Anyone visiting Paris is struck by the mania for *franglais* – the way the French pick up allegedly Anglo-American habits and fill their language with hybrid English words: *le drink, le shopping, le*

War veterans' associations hold doggedly together, recalling French military exploits in two World Wars, Indo-China and North Africa.

Blue collar worker

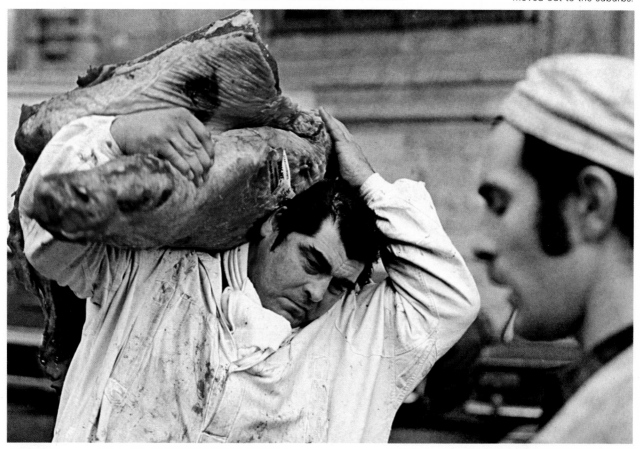

recordman, le management, etc. Young people wear English fashions and listen to Anglo-American pop music. Parisians, always so defensive about their own language, have finally become resigned to speaking English, where previously their pride in French would have prevented them, even if they could. Above all, Paris is being filled with 'pubs,' with little relation to a real London pub, and with 'drugstores' that have even less in common with their American originals. These are simply modern-style Parisian *brasseries* with elaborate hybrid menus and multiple boutiques open till well after midnight. They are patronized by middle-class Parisians, and remain distinctly French. The 'drugstores' are not merely imitations but genuine French creations with a real Parisian style. French taste persists, despite everything.

Paris is a more moral city than London or New York, although, as in many countries, church-going is declining. Only about 12 per cent of Parisians now attend Mass each Sunday. The bourgeoisie will still use the church for baptisms, weddings and funerals, but only in certain *milieux* of society is it required to be a regular church-goer. Christian faith has thus become more sincere, less hypocritical and less widespread. Together with this goes a growing sexual freedom and tolerance, especially among the young. But the old cliché about 'wicked Paris' has always been misleading. The notoriously libertine worlds of Pigalle and the left-bank bohemia were tiny minorities and although the rest of France engaged in *amours* too they did so secretly, within the framework of a rigid Catholic puritanism. Today London, Copenhagen, Hamburg and many other cities have superseded Paris as capitals of promiscuity. The average young Parisian is far more likely to go a virgin to the altar than her London counterpart. French attitudes to birth-control illustrate this *pudeur*. Although the ban on contraceptives was recently lifted relatively few French women yet avail themselves of this new freedom, and abortion is still illegal. The reticence is not religious. Even an agnostic may suffer from an inherent sexual guilt, the legacy of centuries of Catholicism and his Latin origin. For a land with such an amorous reputation, its people are extraordinarily shy and inhibited about sex. These inhibitions are more deep-rooted among working-class women, many of whom are Communist, than in the bourgeoisie.

Like the middle-class the Parisian working-class is torn between old habits and new material aspirations – especially when it has to adapt to a new kind of suburban living. Although there are still slums in Paris, at least half 83

Bourgeoisie

(Top) Parisian husbands are mostly more active in the household than British or American counterparts. And they know a lot about food.

(Above) Off to work on a light breakfast of coffee and rolls to be at his desk by 8 am, father hugs his daughter. Formal school begins age 6.

(Center) Adapting to life in a cramped apartment is a common skill among young middle class families in the overcrowded capital.

(Above) Once a man felt neglected if his wife did not labor over delicate *plats mijotés*. Now a simple grill and a salad will suffice.

Bourgeoisie

the working-class families have been rehoused since the war, mostly in austere high-rise suburban dormitories. The housing shortage, described only ten years ago as 'national disgrace number one', is now steadily being solved. Parisian workers are better off than ever before; unemployment is slight. They spend their money on cars – France's level of car ownership is the highest in Europe after Sweden – on TV sets – the level here has nearly caught up with that in Britain and West Germany – and other such luxuries. They are giving up their old blue working 'uniform' and now dress like the bourgeoisie. Girls wear chic little dresses bought in the big chain stores. It is no longer possible to distinguish between classes by appearance alone. Few of the old traditional working-class pastimes survive. The habit of heavy drinking in cafés is declining. Only rarely can one see some survival from folklore, such as old men playing *boules* in public squares. As in many cities, where people have been moved out of their slum dwellings into new flats with modern luxuries, Parisian workers are not entirely contented. They find it difficult to adapt to new surroundings and make new social contacts, and wives tend to be lonely in the suburbs, despite the clean air and comfort. Some of them even regret the familiar faces and human warmth of their old desolate dwellings. The suburbs have not yet acquired a soul.

While more Parisians are enjoying this increased prosperity, the gulf between rich and poor grows wider. This contrast is particularly marked in Paris, more so than in cities with a greater proportion of unskilled workers. Older or single people are the hardest hit, or those in declining industries. Young couples with children have an advantage, for in an effort to sustain her high birth-rate, France offers the highest family allowances in Europe. Allowances for an average working family with two children will amount to about half the husband's wages. Baby-rearing has become a prestige industry in post-war France, as in Russia. But for the old or handicapped, or other unproductive minorities, the state has less concern. Old-age pensions are among the lowest in any advanced country. Traditionally, old people were provided for by their children and often lived with them; but with the decline of the extended family this custom is dying out. More than 30 per cent of old

People now go to mass less because it is expected than for sincere belief. Children are still entrusted to the care of *les bonnes soeurs*.

Gastronomy survives, as does the old rivalry between the delights of *haute cuisine* and concern for the liver – hence the bottle of mineral water.

After London's Stock
Exchange the Bourse in Paris
is Europe's busiest money
market. Unlike the US,
share owning is not general.

Bourgeoisie

people live quite alone, in poverty. Others may live in special homes where they may be treated as second-class citizens. France is far from being a perfect Welfare State. Hospitals in Paris are less overcrowded than they used to be, but still tend to be bureaucratic and impersonal. The prison system urgently needs reform. Prisons are often filthy, antiquated and barbaric. Added to this, the complexities and delays of the French legal system make life unreasonably tough, to both minor delinquents and hardened lags. With no law of *habeas corpus,* a suspect may remain behind bars for a year or more before any charge is brought against him.

One social problem from which Paris suffers little compared with Britain or America is that of racial tension. Most of the half-million or so Algerian workers in France live in Paris, but there is rarely trouble between them and the French, despite the legacy of Franco-Algerian bitterness. Nor is there any difficulty among south European immigrant workers, Portuguese and others. There are few negroes in Paris, but even if they were more numerous they would probably be well treated. The French are not racists. They ignore foreigners, but rarely victimize them.

One rather large minority that has noisily provoked a great deal of ill-feeling in Paris recently is youth. Though the class-war in Paris has arrived at a wary *status quo,* the generation-war is more savage than in Britain, and nearly as savage as in the United States. Until recently Parisian youth seemed passive and obedient to its parents, more attracted by pop stars than rebel leaders behind barricades. But the student explosion of 1968 has changed much, revealing the discontent that was smouldering beneath the surface. Though the universities have largely settled down again, many Paris *lycées* are in chaos. Classroom discipline, formerly so severe, has been shattered. Teachers are publicly ridiculed or shouted down and work is suffering. Schools have swung from extreme authoritarianism to extreme licence. This is the major anxiety for middle-class parents today, much greater than the physical problems of living in Paris. Within each family, the long established strict authority of parents is now in question. Some teenagers are still meek, while others rebel openly, are outrageously rude, or disappear from home for days on end. LSD, pot, and other drugs are making their belated entry onto the Paris teenage scene and adding to the other worries.

But by no means all young people are disorderly anarchists. Many have a courageous and thoughtful vision of the kind of society they would like to create. They are beginning to revolt against consumer greed, social injustice, and against the still archaic structures of so much of French life. There is much energy and idealism in Parisian youth. How well Parisian society will be able to weather its present transition phase – to become truly modern without sacrificing the best of its civilization – will depend largely on this new generation.

The genteelness of the old
can mask chill penury.
And with close friendships
often contained only within
families, loneliness is common.

The Basques
Spain and France

The Basques, descended from
a Pyrenean Stone Age race,
have the highest incidence
of rhesus negative blood
of any race in the world.

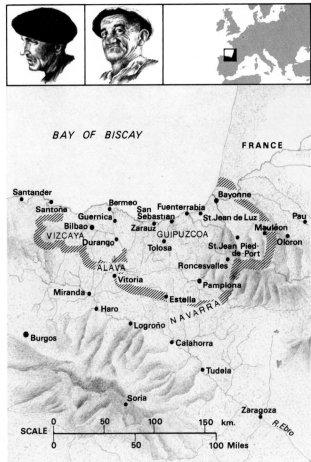

BAY OF BISCAY

FRANCE

Santander
Santoña
Bermeo San Fuenterrabia
Guernica Sebastián
Bilbao Zarauz
VIZCAYA Durango GUIPUZCOA
Tolosa
ALAVA
Vitoria
Miranda Estella
Haro
Logroño NAVARRA
Burgos Calahorra
Tudela
Soria
Zaragoza
R. Ebro

Bayonne
St. Jean de Luz Pau
Mauléon
St. Jean Pied- Oloron
de-Port
Roncesvalles
Pamplona

SCALE
0   50   100   150 km.
0   50   100 Miles

Running along the Spanish shores of the Bay of
Biscay and extending north to Bayonne in France
is a hilly, luxuriant country. The prosperous,
rugged people who live there call it *Euzkadi* – the ancient
homeland of *Eskualdunak*. This is the country we know
as the land of the Basques. Although they are subject to
the laws either of Spain or France, the Basques see themselves as a race apart; and to *Euzkadi* they give their real
allegiance.

The Basque country is divided into seven provinces.
Three are French – Soule, Labourd and Basse-Navarre –
and four Spanish – Vizcaya, Guipúzcoa, Alava and
Navarra. Each province has unique characteristics, but
the strongest contrast is between the French provinces
and the Spanish. The Basque provinces in France seem
very much part of southern Europe; there the physical
aspects of Basque culture – the farms, folk-dances, feasts
– appear slightly self-conscious and theatrical. Lacking
mineral resources and bound to an infertile soil, these
provinces belong to one of the poorest regions of France.
The half million Spanish Basques, on the other hand, live
in one of the most active, advanced areas of Spain. The 89

The Basques Spain and France

(Top) The Basques are Spain's most industrially advanced people. Their region is one of the richest, busiest areas of Spain.

(Center) In St Jean de Luz, Basque fishermen repair their boats. Their ancestors were whalers, pirates and global circumnavigators.

In the Bay of Biscay — where storms are notoriously sudden — Basque fishermen haul in tons of tuna, anchovies and sardines.

vitality and ingeniousness of the Basques have played an important role in shaping Spanish history. Elcano, the first person to circumnavigate the globe, was a Basque. So was Zumalacárregui, the unconquerable leader of the movement that tried to place Don Carlos on the Spanish throne during the last century.

The Basques are thought to have lived in their present area longer than any other race in Europe; their origins are unknown. They are unique as a race: physical anthropologists have shown the Basques to have a lower incidence of blood type B and a higher incidence of blood type O than any other European group. Moreover, Basque blood has the highest incidence of rhesus-negative of any race in the world. In the 18th century the Abbé Lahetjuzan, with typical Basque pride, proved that Adam and Eve were the first Basques. Modern theorists think they are probably descended from a Stone Age race who lived in the Pyrenees and were later modified by the invasions of the Iberian peninsula.

The Basque language, till recently only oral, further complicates the problem. It shows no concrete similarity to any other surviving language. The difficulty of

The French Basque provinces are poor in minerals and in soil: this pair of shaggy cattle are the pride of the show.

Basque grammar is legendary. The language is almost devoid of abstract terms. It has a word for every tree in the Basque provinces, yet no general word for 'tree.' The language has many oddities which linguists find impossible to explain. Another 18th century abbot argued that Basque was the first language spoken by God. However, more sober evidence shows that Basque may be related to languages in the Caucasus mountains of the USSR.

The first reliable historical information on the Basques comes from the 12th century when these people, then renowned for their ill-nature, were described as a mainly pastoral people with some settled agriculture. The chronicler Giraldus Cambrensis in 1120 portrays them as 'thirsty for blood and ferocious as the wild beast with which they live.'

Basque history is dominated by their struggle on the one hand to maintain their autonomy and distinctive way of life; and their gradual submission on the other to the governments that have ruled them and the forces of progress which have changed them economically. These two themes are encapsulated in the history of the Basque *fueros*.

The *fueros* were charters granted in the Middle Ages to particular provinces and districts which allowed the people complete local autonomy in return for their allegiance to the kings of either Castile or France. The *fueros,* proclaimed at first by word of mouth, were gradually expanded and codified until they covered all the laws and customs that regulated every aspect of Basque life. The privileges granted by the *fueros* enabled the Basques to have their own courts of law, parliaments, coinage and militia. Each province elected a governing assembly. Without its consent no order of the king was valid. The administration of the Basque provinces was notably efficient and uncorrupt. The kings of Spain swore to uphold the Basque liberties under the venerable oak tree of Guernica, the symbolic capital of the Basque race and the city later famous for being so heinously devastated during the Spanish Civil War.

As time passed the centralizing tendencies of both the French and Spanish monarchies increasingly clashed with the *fueros* which protected Basque regional autonomy. The French Basques lost their liberties in the French Revolution. Navarre was deprived of her *fueros* in 1840 as punishment for supporting Don Carlos in his first attempt to become King of Spain, and the other three Spanish provinces underwent the same fate after the 2nd Carlist War. But the *fueros* were never forgotten and are crucial to our understanding of the Basques. Today the principle of *fueros* is a prime mover behind Basque separatist sentiments.

Basque separatist arguments are reinforced economically by the swelling industrial strength of the Basque

The Basques are the only people in the world to use this complex contraption, which is a device for weighing cows.

The Basques Spain and France

The Basques are famous wine-makers. A man at work has a skin of wine with him. The occasional swig makes the day go better.

These men speak a language that has no link with any other, save for similarities between Basque and one of the Caucasus languages.

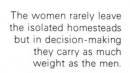

In the 19th century the Russian anarchist Prince Bakunin was inspired by the Basque farmers and their self-reliant hill communities.

The women rarely leave the isolated homesteads but in decision-making they carry as much weight as the men.

provinces. Industry is gaining an increasing hold on the economic life of the Basques, although fishing, agriculture, animal husbandry and smuggling have for centuries been the backbone of the Basque economy. Basque economic stamina is securely founded on their industriousness and thrift. Although their strong sense of regional identity makes them politically insular, economically they are unrestrainedly out-going.

Basque whalers may have prospered in the Bay of Biscay as early as the 10th century. By the 13th and 14th centuries whale fishing had become a Basque monopoly. In search of whales and cod, the Basques traveled as far as Labrador, Greenland and Hudson's Bay. Rumor has it that a captain of a Basque whaling boat discovered America before Columbus. Their boats were certainly large enough to make the voyage; and they had a great knowledge of seafaring. During the numerous wars between Spain and France their whaling ports including San Juan de Luz and Biarritz were destroyed. Eventually the Basques were expelled from their traditional whaling waters. But even before their expulsion they had found with their usual ingenuity another profitable outlet for their maritime skills – piracy. As pirates (and as slavers, too) they were as successful as they had been as whalers.

The separatism of the Basques persists partly because they live in wild hill country far from the swim of French or Spanish life.

Their athletic dances here performed in Pamplona, owe nothing to the culture of France or Spain. The Basques are a race apart.

In the ancient Basque city of Pamplona a man competing in a traditional contest raises a stone that weighs 247 pounds.

(Bottom) Basques gamble heavily on contests like this ram fight, which is a favorite spectacle in the port of San Sebastian.

Fishing is still of major importance: they haul in tons of tuna, anchovies and sardines.

But the Basques are mainly a rural people. The agriculture of the Basque provinces is mixed and intensive. Their methods of working the land are varied, the fields are rarely left fallow. Among their crops are wheat, corn, beans, rye, grapes and alfalfa – which is turned into hay. There are also fruit and nut trees – apple, pear, chestnut and walnut. The land is steep and divided into many plots; simple tools are the most useful and modern farming machinery is rare. In typical Basque farms there are cows and sheep for commercial use, pigs and chickens for home consumption. Because of the nature of the terrain and the harshness of the soil, more and more land is turned over to pine forest for long-term profit.

The three-storied Basque farmstead, the *baserria,* is the basic unit and shapes the character of Basque rural life. It always has a name and its history is known in detail. So closely is the family identified with the farmstead that the family is known by the name of the house in which it lives. The family sees the *echea,* or household – the main dwelling, household furnishings, outbuildings, land holdings, farming tools and the site on the floor of the village church – as immoveable and timeless. The family which belongs to the *echea* may change, but the

echea itself must be handed down through the generations or sold intact. The permanency of the *echea* gives Basque rural society its continuity. To break or divide it up is thought morally offensive and economically foolish.

Each *baserria* is grouped with others into a neighborhood called the *auzoa* which has its own chapel, road system, patron saint, and mayor. *Auzoa* members often see each other and co-operate for the common good. The *auzoak* (the plural of *auzoa*) are arranged around a village nucleus of religious and secular organizations which provide essential services. Personal contacts beyond the *auzoa* are rare and when they exist often formal, respectful, cold and slightly tinged with suspicion. The rural Basque belongs above all to the *baserria.*

Ideally the *baserria* is occupied by only one domestic group: an elderly semi-retired married couple, a young and active married couple and the unmarried children of both. Members of the household are usually related by blood and must live on the farmstead. Relations between members of the domestic group are affectionate, close and respectful. Husband and wife usually refer to each other by the polite 'thee,' as do the children when they address their parents. As soon as a member who is not the heir to the farm marries, he or she loses all rights to the *echea* although warm ties remain. Co-operation is essential and highly valued on the *baserria* which is

94

Basques are fine dancers.
In the plaza of an old
Basque town in the
Pyrenees, enthusiasts
dance on after dusk.

The Basques Spain and France

Basques are staunch Roman Catholics but ancient superstition persists. They fear Satan — and the mythical cave-dwelling *laminak* dwarves.

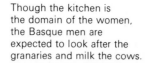

Though the kitchen is the domain of the women, the Basque men are expected to look after the granaries and milk the cows.

When a Basque girl marries, she leaves the family homestead and renounces all rights of inheritance.

almost an autonomous and self-sufficient unit. The Basques rarely visit each other casually. Outsiders hardly ever enter the house.

The kitchen is the woman's domain; the stables and granaries are the man's. Outside the house both sexes share the chores. Basque women are not judged inferior to men; nor are their positions of less consequence. When important decisions are taken equal weight is given to the opinions of both husband and wife. No decision is taken without a consensus. In Basque society, unlike the rest of France and especially Spain, there is no double standard in sexual behavior. Men and women are equally bound by a strict moral code. Unmarried mothers are censured but not ostracized; illegitimate children are not despised. But it is true that men enjoy more freedom, because they are more active and social outside the *baserria*.

The basic core of the family is the *echekojaun* and *echekoandria* – the *baserria*'s young active couple. They are tied by Basque society's strongest emotional bond and carry the responsibility for the continuing success of the *baserria*. The ideal *echekojaun* (husband) is hardworking, dignified, serious and thrifty – attributes valued throughout Basque society. His wife mirrors these qualities and is also intensely loyal and conscientious in her religious duties. Since the farm, to remain profitable, must not be broken up, only one child can succeed to the ownership of the *echea,* although all children have equal rights to the personal wealth of their parents. Male primogeniture is preferred, but the *echea* usually passes to the child, male or female, who is thought most suitable. When the selected heir is married he inherits the legal rights to the *baserria*; the parents remain on the farm but usually in well-earned retirement. The brothers or sisters of the heir are compensated with money from the household reserves. They can then make a suitable marriage at another farm, or start a different life in the cities or in the New World.

Class structure is hard to define in rural Basque life as equality is an outstanding feature of Basque culture. Among the Basques only people who let their *baserria* deteriorate or sell part of their inheritance are treated with ridicule and scorn. But one division does run deep. It creates two opposing and often conflicting groups. This is the division between Basque and non-Basque.

The Basques are a reserved, independent and insular people; they never fully accept a stranger in their society. The Basques say 'The hand of the stranger is heavy.' No matter how long he has lived on Basque soil, he is always greeted with some mistrust and resentment. He is thought inferior and corrupt. The foreigner is of course usually Spanish or French and regarded as a usurper. The Basques have a strong belief in their racial superiority. The reasons are not hard to find. The vast influx of immigrants from the rest of Spain and France has changed the character of traditional Basque life. The

96

In Basque houses animals and people live together, the people on the middle and top floors, the livestock on the bottom.

The Basques' strong sense of equality means that labor is shared. There are no class differences — only the gulf between Basque and non-Basque.

Basques think it has been a change for the worse.

There are three physical objects, visible everywhere, which give the Basque countryside its special character: the *frontón*, the walled court where *jai-alai* (pelota) – which typifies the robust outdoor life of the Basque – is played by striking a hard ball against the wall with a wickerwork racquet; the cemetery with its respect for tradition; and the church – symbol of the fervent faith of the Basques. The Basques are completely Roman Catholic, fully accept Catholic doctrine and have an ardent literal belief in the Bible. There are religious rituals for every major stage in the life cycle.

But although the Basques are profoundly Christian, their supernatural world is inhabited by malevolent spirits, flying fire-breathing serpents, ominous messengers and witches. The folk literature is rich in tales of the deeds of these supernatural figures; superstition is still important in the daily life of the rural Basques. The mischievous behavior of the *laminak,* a race of small cave-dwelling people, often causes havoc in the field and house. The curses of evil-eyed witches can entice wicked spirits to enter the bodies of enemies, causing pain and disease. Elaborate rituals and countless superstitions are associated with death. Occasionally the wandering souls of the departed can be heard trying to make contact with the people of the earth.

97

Bretons
France

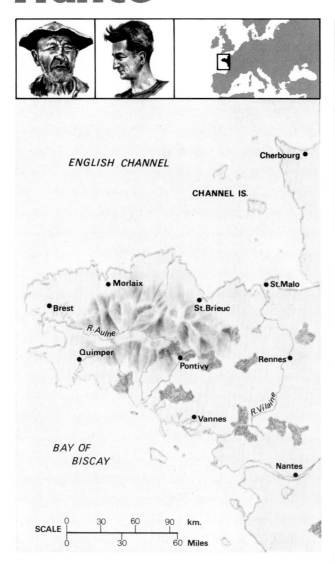

ENGLISH CHANNEL

Cherbourg ●

CHANNEL IS.

● Morlaix

● St.Malo

● Brest

St.Brieuc

R. Aulne

● Quimper

Pontivy

Rennes ●

R. Vilaine

● Vannes

BAY OF
BISCAY

Nantes

SCALE 0 ____ 30 ____ 60 ____ 90 km.
        0 _____ 30 _____ 60 Miles

Old Breton men and women have a mystical past which recalls both their Celtic history and their isolation from the rest of France. It is in their blood and they view the 20th century with a mixture of awe and perplexity. The changes that have been brought to France in the last 100 years have only discovered Brittany in the space of the past couple of generations. Here the conflict between old and new is most profound.

There are old people who, in isolated villages, reckon the past as synonymous with barbarity. They are a short, dark and wiry people who talk of the days when people constantly fought one another, when there were many thieves and rogues and when the life of the peasant was as harsh as it was simple. Men were day laborers or tenant farmers; women were drudges in tiny, one roomed *pentys,* the traditional one-storied stone farmhouse. The passing of those days few regret; but if a new and improved standard of living has come, there is also

99

Brittany's past is cherished
by the older women who
worship at shrines like the
15th century stone chapel of
Notre Dame de Tronoën.

Horses and carts bring the seaweed, collected in the boats, to the shore. Tiny coastal villages often have no harbor.

the nostalgia for other old ways – the festivals, dances and betrothals, the telling of old legends around the hearth when the family gathered together; and the respect once owed by all to the father as the patriarch. These are things that pass.

In a small Breton village in the moorlands you can still witness the remnant of another world. On a Sunday the people flock to church to take mass and gossip with their neighbors. Old men wear round hats and black tunics buttoned at the side; and their shoes are wooden and varnished. The older women wear tall, cylindrical coiffe hats of white lace, and aprons over ample black skirts. On other days in the week the village still seems apart from the century. After nightfall it is soon quiet, streets are deserted and windows are dark. The village sleeps at an hour when Paris and Parisians are awake. *Buvettes*

Heavy Atlantic seas and strong winds batter the Breton coast. Sudden squalls spring up to menace an offshore fishing smack.

The kelp (a seaweed) from the low tide mark raked up by this old woman will fertilize the land. Kelp ash used to be sold for its iodine content.

and bars are long empty of the muted whispers of old men huddled round a table with glasses of red wine. Their rural life does not extend beyond the light of day.

Older Bretons are people of an ancient mold. Often they will not accept the conveniences of a modern world. Running water, electricity and gas are things, they say, not of their age. And in many ways they are right. Many of the people have not emerged from the traditions of the past, the ways of two generations ago that seem to the outsider like the ways of medieval times. There are a few old women who have never been more than a short distance from their hamlet, who do not speak French and who will not believe the world is round and travels round the sun. They feel safer with candles and oil lamps and pulling water from a well.

But their children grow into a world of schools, reading and writing, and an atomic power station close to the village. Boys grow their hair long, ride motor-cycles and mingle with girls in mini-skirts, careless of their parents, at discothèques and dances. Education brings to the young a new awareness of their parents' and grand-parents' backwardness.

Until World War II Britanny had been isolated from the body of France. A rugged peninsula of moorland and rocky coastland, where farming was hard – the small-holdings scattered among rocky valleys and on the moorlands, where meager crops of vegetables and wheat and barley were grown – and fishing an uncertain industry on the wind-swept coast; it was a place ideal for a near feudal society. The transformation which, in De Gaulle's words, allowed Bretons to 'marry their century' brought greater equality, but also side-effects that were insidious to traditionalists.

Bretons are people of the Celtic fringe. Their ancestors were Cornishmen who migrated to this part of France more than a thousand years ago (Britanny was also called Cornouailles) and brought with them much of their Celtic language and customs. Breton traditions and idioms, relics from antiquity, have changed little. They have the ancient Celtic tradition of oral literature, spoken over fires in the *pentys* when the family gathered together to listen to the tales of the itinerant tailor. And the festivals, the *pardons,* which were events of great importance in the Breton calendar.

In all *pardons* there is something in their air of mystic-ism and piety of the ancient Celtic. A tourist may see them only as a show, but it goes far deeper than that. In the past all Breton life was wrapped up in the *pardons.* Marriages were arranged and the older people looked on as the younger ones played their part. There is a pro-cession from a village to a remote chapel where, perhaps, the tomb of an old saint is visited. After prayers there are games, dances and singing, much in the Welsh or Irish tradition. At Rumengol, which is crowded on *pardon* days, there is still told the old legend of Gralon, King of Cornwall, who was buried there by a monk and a druid. 101

(Left) When this woman was
young only the 'finished' old
face was thought beautiful.
Now her face is distinguished
by a stubborn shrewdness.

Two old Breton fishermen, who
rarely take off their blue
berets, play an informal
game of *boules* with others
from their village.

(Center) A Breton farm or
smallholding is often no larger
than 20 acres. All the family
help with the plowing,
sowing and reaping.

He is a kind of local saint and about his tomb the *pardon*
is centered.

Thirty years ago, throughout Brittany, the *pardons*
were attended by almost all, from the oldest to the
youngest. Somehow they confirmed the Breton identity,
separate from the rest of France. They were steeped in a
world quite apart from the harshness of day to day life.
But as other things change; as old men are no longer
accorded the respect, obedience and veneration of
patriarchs; so too old customs lose their appeal for the
young. Wisdom and experience are not to be found
among the traditions and people of a by-gone age; the
children find them in schools and large towns, in books
and factories. Modern life holds more promise of
adventure.

For the older Bretons it's another symptom of the
relentlessly changing world. Women who were guardians
of the age-old cult of the dead, preserving the most
solemn tradition of Celtic pre-history, ask the dead to
share in their astonishment: 'I'd like the people who died
fifty years ago to come back and see . . .' But as well as
seeming the protectors of old values and one step behind
the men, the women are also ambivalent in their attitude.
In their long lives they have had less contact with the encroachments of the modern world; they are more
religious; many speak only Breton and wear only
traditional clothes, and some will never enter a *buvette*
to take a glass of wine. But a lifetime of practicality
allows them to accept and even push their men into
acquiring domestic conveniences. When the man has
sunk into alcoholism, it is the woman who takes over all
responsibilities. It is significant that among Breton men
there is the highest incidence of that malady in all France.

The older women have come from an age that regarded
the ancient and wrinkled face as the truly beautiful: the
beauty of wisdom. Young faces were unfinished – which
contrasts with the modern conception of beauty only in
the young. Yet this they have accepted just as they have
accepted the changes in their homes. Where once the
penty was only a single room in which hearth and
benches, dresser and bed were closeted together, now the
separation of living from sleeping and eating from
cooking is common. Women allow the domestic revolution to enter their homes. A fire-place is replaced by a
stove – and the old polarization of the family round the
hearth is lost.

The story-teller who once held spellbound a cluster of
fathers and sons, mothers and daughters with his tales
of Celtic legend – perhaps the tale of Iseult arriving from
Ireland to find her Tristan dead, or of Merlin in the
forest of Broceliande – is now replaced by the fairy-tales
of television, spun through the air. For this, families need
not gather together; they need not preserve their Celtic
legends for cold evenings sheltered from the outside. The
price they pay for progress takes much of their inheritance away.

103

The *pardon*, an old festival
to commemorate local saints
often only attended by the
older women. Here a pro-
cession visits a rocky shrine.

The industrial north
England

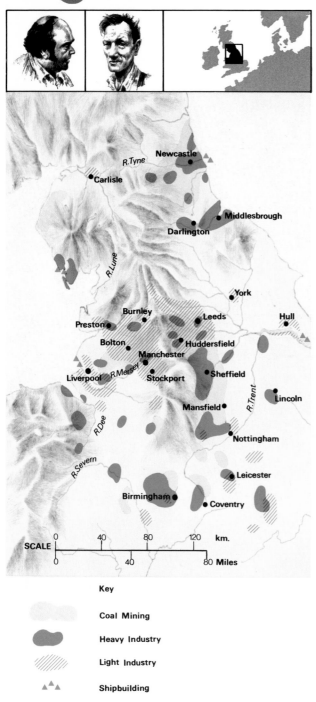

SCALE

| 0 | 40 | 80 | 120 | km. |

| 0 | 40 | | 80 | Miles |

Key

Coal Mining

Heavy Industry

Light Industry

Shipbuilding

In the south of England, in the Home Counties around London, people have no very distinct ideas about the north: it is a grey mass of territory somewhere up the railway lines from Euston and St Pancras stations; it is a bit colder and foggier; there is a lot of coal, factories, a large lumpen proletariat speaking in flat accents, often a bit coarse and cussed; the young from the north when they come south seem on the awkward side, a bit too

105

Whippet racing, an old working
class sport, thrives today.
The dogs are pets too and
cheerfully known as 'poor
man's greyhounds.

A northern smog blurs a townscape in Yorkshire, built in granite and slate when the coal and wool industries flourished.

blunt, even shy. They would be mostly surprised to know that Nottingham is nearer to London than to Glasgow. But in the north most people have got quite clear ideas about London and the south-easterners generally. That is where the money is made, the strings are pulled, where the fast talkers and the over-educated get away with it, and where most of the solid wealth for which the hard work of the north is responsible is manipulated and spent. In hotter countries like Italy and Brazil, the cooler parts tend to be the heads and the warmer parts the bodies. In France the relationship of the northern industrial belt to Paris is more that of Birmingham and Coventry to the south-east rather than the north to the south-east. The English 'north' hugs to itself its own attitudes and achievements.

There is a joke in the repertory of the Manchester comedian Les Dawson which defines working class humor in the north of England. His speciality is a delicious gloom in the disastrous business of being alive. With his sad, fat face registering a belligerent self-pity he tells his audience that he doesn't claim his family was the poorest in the street. But what he will say is that until he was 16 he thought knives and forks were jewelry.

Exaggerating poverty, deprivation and the ignorance that goes with them, especially when describing your own background or prospects, is a folk art in the industrial north of England. A stand-up comic like Dawson is a kind of public grumbler, or official pessimist who is enthusiastically supported at the box office to celebrate the drudgery of people's lives, and by monstrously caricaturing it to defeat it.

Not that the lives of the northern industrial worker and his family are a perpetual struggle against squalor and toil. Today in this region of about seventeen million people there is great variety in working conditions, housing, incomes, educational standards, leisure activity and sheer local character. Changes have been rapid since World War II ended. But there is an abiding image of The North, real both to those who live there and those who don't, and that is the oppressiveness of its past. Writers, painters and reformers have all depicted northern working class life as harsh and underprivileged – a generalization undeniable until only a generation ago. The north believes, with some justice, in its toughness, endurance, ill fortune and non-equivocation. That is the northern tradition.

Coal, textiles, engineering, shipbuilding, iron and steel have dominated and conditioned the lives of people in the north for more than a century. And although methods and products have changed, they still do. There are thousands fewer coal miners than there were twenty years ago. The Lancashire cotton industry moves steadily to the dubious state of antiquity. The entire north-east talks uncertainly of the future of its shipyards. But plant for motor manufacture, electrical components, industrial chemicals and household appliances have been introduced and the north has lost none of its sense of being the workshop of England, a relationship comparable to that of the Ruhr to Germany. A stranger at a social club or public house in a mining village or housing estate will feel excluded by nothing more foreign than the reiterated *argot* of work. Among these people who make things, handle tools and mind machines manual skills and mechanical processes pervade their most casual conversation.

In the major re-housing programmes since World War II in every town thousands of families have been moved out of the old, often miserably squalid streets close to the factories. Now they live in tower blocks or municipal apartments or in regimental lines of brick boxes on the urban fringes. Communities of families

Budgerigars, dogs and racing
pigeons (especially among
cooped up coalminers) are
the favorite pets among northern
working class families.

Nowadays new council estates
are preferred to solidly built
terraces like those in Salford,
Lancashire, quite acceptable
up to the 1950s.

107

In the wasteland of rubble
created by slum clearance
schemes, a little girl
builds a home of her
own.

The Salvation Army — offering gospel music, poor relief and Christian charity — grew out of the urban misery of the industrial revolution.

which used to be tightly grouped according to the industries they worked in have now been fragmented. Mill operatives, office clerks, laborers and craftsmen now live together on new housing estates in a way unknown before when the employee paid his rent to his employer-landlord. But where there is one dominating industry such as steel in Sheffield or Scunthorpe even the modern estates with their well-tended gardens, family cars and the odd sailing dinghy on its blocks in the garage evince the community feeling that comes from the ties of the works canteen, the same union, the same wages, the same training, the same future.

This kind of shared experience and inter-dependence are at their most evident in the mining communities – just as one finds in Belgium's Borinage or the West Virginia coalfields. In a coal-mining village like Brodsworth in south Yorkshire there is a sense of allegiance and of common roots. There is a common commitment and a common lack of choice. It is particularly affecting that this allegiance should be directed to an industry which is the most dramatic example of recent industrial change: now the pits need fewer men; they are increasingly mechanized, and the future of every pit is forseeably circumscribed.

Pride is too easy and sentimental a word to explain the miners' attitude. In fact many miners view their jobs with dislike and fear. Even now the pits kill and maim their men. In a mining community going down the pits is almost a compulsion. Steve, for example, a 20-year-old with secondary school attainments which qualify him for training in many less arduous careers explains his job in the pit with apologetic resignation: 'My mother kept telling me I was screwy for coming down here. The pit's got a stigma, I know. But my father's a miner, so was my grandfather.'

There is too among this young generation of miners an exuberant relish for the comparatively high level of wages a skilled man can quickly reach. The fashionable long hair and above-ground colorful clothing of the young miners seem startlingly inappropriate in the somber northern streets. A 19-year-old apprentice pit electrician, with hair to his shoulders, a motor-bike on which he zooms with his girl at 80 miles an hour, who plans to tour Italy and Switzerland with her and some friends in a caravan, was studying two days a week at a technical college and expected to earn between $30 and $50 a week within a year. He said: 'I don't think it's really hard work. You just don't have to mind being under the ground a lot.'

Like others of his generation, who often have a gentle compassion for the exhaustion and ill-treatment suffered by their fathers, he had no illusions about what life in the pits would have been like had he been born 20 years earlier. He had heard plenty of the bitter, recent memories of his father's generation. Bill, aged 48, with two sons in the pit, recalled that as recently as the early

(Above) In a good week a stripper can make £100 ($240) in a working men's club. Most of her lunch-time audience have been on night shift.

(Below) Five o'clock and the end of the day shift for automobile workers at Chorley in Lancashire. Shifts are organised by rota.

'sixties he was still filling the coal-waggons by hand. 'I remember throwing it up eight feet with a shovel. That was really horsework.' He had gone underground immediately when he left school at 14. He worked with ponies and carried chains across his shoulders to hook coal waggons on to an endless rope. His first pay day ever came after the first time he worked six shifts in a week. Now he operated a power-loading machine. But he still did not earn as much as the 19-year-old electrician with a technical qualification. The young miners had 'never worked' Bill said, relief for them and resentment over his own experience conflicting in his voice.

He supposed he should feel lucky that mechanization had probably extended his working life in the pit to the age of 60. 'Without it I'd have had to stop by now – by the time I was 50, for sure.' His elder son felt the same bonds with the pit as his father. When he left school he aimed to train as a chef. When that chance fell through he went straight down the mines without even considering an alternative.

There is a self-sufficiency about the village. There are men's clubs for ex-servicemen, gardeners, fishing enthusiasts and racing pigeon owners. Better wages and working conditions have put new life into pigeon-racing. Against this grimy narrowness of the dark pit, pigeons are small soft angels. Men can now breed them more ex-

pensively and go for bigger prize money. A pair of good birds can cost as much as $63. But it has reduced the traditional interest in racing whippets because, as someone explained 'with full employment there isn't time to exercise the dogs.'

Still, on a Sunday afternoon at a recreation field among grey-green misted hills there are three stone shelters, two sets of football posts and, in a roped-off stretch of ground, whippets are racing; the poor man's greyhound racing; the traditional working man's hobby. The owners are screaming their names and waving rags. As a race ends the dogs hurtle into their owners' arms. An old woman shouts 'We've won!'

The old men of the village, retired miners, are sent to the sea-side every year by public subscription with 'two good meals, a pound each to spend, and a cigar.' A muscular, but undemonstrative masculinity dominates the village. Few women go out to work. Their job is to look after the men.

On the north-east coast, where pay and self-confidence fluctuate with the fortunes of the shipyards and heavy engineering plants, the prestige of the male is proclaimed in a more strident style. Here the more austere institutions of local tradition, the old clubs intended for evening drinking, darts and dominoes with occasional concerts by brass bands or male voice choirs, have given way to a newer, brasher kind of club.

There is one club where a packed audience watches a strip show every Monday lunchtime – when work is plentiful. It has a three-sided gallery bar overlooking the stage and main room, and an audience of night-workers and other men who had simply not bothered to turn up for work. The stripper, a former petrol pump girl, worked the northern clubs and said she preferred the ones in the north-east because they paid best. She expected to make $100 in a good week. 'They're the hardest audiences up here' she said. 'They expect more. I usually give them a French maid.'

Committees of working men run the clubs, each with a 'concerts secretary,' whose determined competitiveness would match that of any London club proprietor. He books the acts on which the club's popularity, prosperity and 'tone' depend. Not every club wants a stripper or a blue comedian. 'I won't have either, not even on a Sunday lunchtime when we don't encourage women' said one concerts secretary. Women should be at home cooking on Sunday mornings.

The coastline of the north-east, in the stretches between the old coal pits and the new cooling towers, can be unforgettably beautiful in its stillness. But it is the kind of area where one is always coming up against reminders of wretchedness. The lone figure, searching along the sea-shore, stuffing lumps of washed-up coal into a sack is 'scrattin' for a living, and will try to sell the bag of coal around the streets for the price of a pound of bacon. The north-east has a stubbornly high rate of un- 109

The industrial north England

Scrubbing the doorstep until it gleams is a daily task for working class wives in the older parts of the towns.

Fish and chips are eaten throughout working Britain. Once wrapped in old newspapers the law now demands paper bags.

employment. This is most worrying when adolescents cannot find a job when they leave school.

One of the club secretaries, a man in his early forties, and an electric welder in a shipyard, seemed to have less sympathy for the figures hunting the beaches than they deserved. 'You've got a lot of people who don't *want* to work' he said as if denying all connection with their misfortune. And one might think him a hard man, smugly self-satisfied in his own modest comfort. Until one hears this story from his childhood: 'Every Friday I used to have to run for my dinner. There were a lot of kids doing the same thing. You ran from school and your mother was standing at the front door at home with a bundle of newspapers. You grabbed them from her, and raced for the fish-and-chip-shop. If you got there first and gave the man the papers he gave you a pile of chips. If you got there second you got nothing.' Attitudes to security and privation are intensely personal. Most people have memorable experiences of both.

By memory or by actual repetition the past obtrudes persistently into the present. There are men who took part in the Hunger Marches from the north-east to London in 1936 when unemployment reached the appalling proportion of 90 per cent in some districts. In London in 1971 the same men were back again protesting about unemployment.

There are also movements in the north-east that are entirely new. A dismissive impatience with what has gone before has produced a new ethic: full employment is not necessarily desirable; in fact any employment at all may be highly undesirable. The phenomenon of the Claimants' and Unemployed Workers' Union, born in a shabby little house on a municipal estate in south Yorkshire in 1970 now has to be treated seriously as a developing pressure group on national government. From this house erupt vehement attacks on cyclostyled handsheets on economic policies that 'deliberately create unemployment' and copious advice to the workless and unemployed on how to squeeze more aid out of the Social Security. Their view is that there is no particular moral virtue in work. If the national economy needs to reduce the labor force then there should be reward, not penalty, for volunteers for unemployment. The low-paid worker should consider whether he would not be better off cleverly manipulating the Social Security regulations so that he can simultaneously stop work and raise his income. It is not surprising that the Claimants' Union gets chilly treatment from the mainstream of politicians. Even in the north's most disillusioned areas the Labour Party's philosophy is based on the advancement of the worker, not of the man who rejects work.

The new anti-work ethic of the Claimants' Union certainly seems eccentric compared with the classical northern working class attitudes. For every young miner who drops out and finds enough money in his dole to smoke an occasional joint there are many more young-

In some of the older coal
mines in Durham, pit ponies
still drag the coal waggons.
But they no longer live
permanently underground.

A young technician in the
mines can earn from £35 (say
$75) to £50 a week. His
father cut coal by hand and
was an old man at 50.

sters like Eileen and Stuart, 21 and 22 respectively, who
live in a Lancashire town which has shifted awkwardly
from a dependence on cotton to a variety of light engineering and know down to the last detail what life will
hold for them. What they have firmly in mind is a stable
future: steady jobs, marriage, their own (not a rented)
house, two children – one of each sex – and no trouble.
They know when they will marry and what their house
will be like. Nothing is likely to deflect them from their
objectives.

Eileen says: 'We're going to get married in a year to
eighteen months, because then we'll have reached our
target to save $1200. That's to put down on one of the
stone-built houses out on the edge of town. It'll cost
about $4800. We thought about a dormer bungalow,
which is what I really want, but they're about $9600. I'm   111

(Left) Blackpool's Golden Mile of sand (just visible here) represents summer holidays, seaside, and saucy fun for working class north.

A Victorian gas lamp stands as a reminder of William Morris' 'vestibule of Hell' – the now cleared slums of central Manchester.

not going to have any children for the first three years, so I can keep my job. Then I want a boy first, then a girl.' She was cheerful and eager about her future, although she could see its deficiences. It was predictable, uneventful, modest. What attracted and even excited her were its security and equilibrium. Now Stuart occasionally took her motor racing and they went into Manchester to a night-club most Saturdays. After marriage she expected most of that going out to stop, and this was, to her, entirely proper.

Six months after her 21st birthday she was still talking about it. It had been such a thrilling week that it was still enough to put a tremble in her voice. There had been a party for 100 guests in an upstairs room of an hotel, dancing to a record player, presents of a gold watch, a leather coat, a bracelet, a camera, an alarm clock and nightgowns: 'Fabulous!' – and she anticipated no future event to equal its glory.

And if Eileen's lack of expectation seems unduly cautious, consider the interjection of her mother whose own 21st birthday fell in the bare days of the late 1940s. 'I got six cups, six saucers and six plates' she said. She was boasting about that frugality, in the northern tradition, with a smile.

West Indians and Bengalis live in Manchester's 'Little Harlem' free of racial conflict. They share the Lancastrian love of cricket.

It's the same the whole world over on a seaside holiday, on reprieve from the daily round of factory shifts and office hours.

Tinkers
Ireland

Tinker women have a distinctive style. They are usually tall and wear their greased hair off the shoulders or in plaits. Under their black or plaid shawls, they place their infants and market supplies and conceal their proceeds from begging. They usually carry a basket under their arm and wear wellingtons or leather boots to signify their connection with horses. The men often sport long sideburns and 'country and western' style of dress with leather lumber jackets which English navvies wear, and the 'Paddy's cap.' Unlike the women, they rarely beg and can blend easily with the poorer Irish society.

People often confuse tinkers with Gypsies. In fact, tinkers are no different in origin from the Irish Celts. Gypsies are said to be of Indian descent and speak Romany. Tinkers are fair-skinned and traditionally speak *Shelte,* a Celtic language. Gypsies claim a unique mythology, background and religion. Tinkers are vague about their origins, but almost all of them are baptized Roman Catholic.

As Gypsies and tinkers both live the life on the road, however, there are certain similarities. Tinkers originally used the salt-box type of caravan or the ass and cart, but later adopted the gypsy barrel-shaped caravan. Both groups prefer piebald horses to pull the flat-car or cart. They all live in tents. As they get richer, they use motorized caravans and lorries for hauling scrap. Other occupations common to both Gypsies and tinkers are fortune-telling, rag-collecting, tin-smithing, carpentry and seasonal work.

The camp of even the most wealthy tinker seems completely disorganized. Babies' bottles, straw bundles and gallon tins are strewn about the central hearth of the tent. The bow-tent widely used in Ireland and Scotland consists of a bunch of wattles smoked into curves and covered with canvas. A hole is left in the center for the smoke to escape. Occasionally a stovepipe and oil drum serve as a makeshift chimney. The kettle hangs from the 'stakes' and every family possesses a few iron pots for cooking 'cabbage and pork of a Sunday.' Bread and tea are the staples of a poor diet sometimes varied with semolina or rice. Tucked away somewhere in the tent there are probably some bundles of clothes stored from charity rounds among settled people who are known as gentry or 'countrymen.' The tinkers also hoard sheets of tin for making mugs or 'ponjers,' plus the tinsmith's tools: anvil, bellows, soldering tongs, snips or clips and hammer.

114 It is suggested that tinkers were once members of a

Tinkers consider traveling
an occupation in itself, but
carry a small forge and other
tools needed for metal-work
in the cart.

The nomadic life of a tinker family, earning its keep by tin-smithing, horse-trading and peddling means that children are often illiterate.

Some tinkers, like this chimney-sweep, do other work and live in houses. Old ways decline — even *Shelte*, their traditionally secret language.

craftsmen élite in feudal Ireland; that they were Druidic bards who occupied an important position in society; that they were Knights of the road, descendants of noble victims of the great Potato Famine which ravaged the people between 1845 and 1849, or the people who were pushed westward during Oliver Cromwell's campaign 'To Hell or to Connaught.' Scholars have yet to be convinced of their origins.

Today tinkers are still fully occupied traveling and begging. Tinsmithing originally forced the tinker to seek work in different places; wandering and metal still go together. In constant competition with the blacksmith's stable pitch, the tinker carried a mobile forge, shod horses and did any other work he could find. But plastic and the craftsman's decline are killing tinsmithing.

There are four classes of tinkers. The lowest groups have few possessions and no caravans. They are usually the first to accept housing under government programs. The second group's children are also illiterate but the group has caravans. The top group is of rich, widely traveling dealers in antiques, scrap and horses. They have motor-caravans and lorries, and speak a smart dialect of

Shelte, the tinker's secret language. This élite has gradually made the clan-oriented system give way to one of scrap-brotherhoods.

Shelte is still a mystery. Said to be a mixture of Bog Latin, Romany, Irish, and spoken with English interpolations, the language is spoken less and less today. Tinkers claim its decline is linked with the death of the tinsmithing trade. They believe *Shelte* is inherited and bears superstitious qualities which will 'solder a pot and mend the tinker's dam,' the latter being a small hole in the ground where sand and solder are blended.

As well as *Shelte* tinkers use *patrin* or signs as a unique medium of communication. Charred embers, sticks or rags are placed in a certain way to indicate the birth of a child, the arrival of a foal, the death of a relative, the generosity of local people, the desire for horses, etc. Affinities have been noted with script in ancient Runic (old Norse) and with designs on archaeological mounds.

Marriages between Gypsies and tinkers are discouraged. The children of these unions are referred to scathingly as 'posh rats,' 'mumpers,' 'didicois,' or half-breeds. The tinker's marriage is carefully arranged by a matchmaker, usually a wealthy member of the community, skilled in making bargains, along with jokes and hugely exaggerated stories. The match-maker invites members of the 'spree' into the tent to discuss the attributes of the future bride and groom, who may never have met and are allowed one 'walk in the field' before the wedding. There is a great deal of inter-marriage.

Marriages between tinkers and the settled community are looked down upon. Such couples will not be able to return to the tinker brides' parents which would be normal after the honeymoon. The children of such a match will be shared out among relations. Often the products of incestuous or 'unlawful' unions are adopted by total outsiders.

Just as marriages take place in church, so do funerals follow the rites of the Catholic church. When a tinker dies (usually before he reaches 60) he is laid out within easy reach of the road. As well as the immediate family of the deceased, which is on average eight-strong, members of distant clans are expected to attend the wake which is punctuated by keeners, mourners and much drinking and singing. The women relatives tear their hair and do not eat, the men blacken their faces and moan. After the wake, which can last several days, the possessions of the deceased are often burned, including their caravan.

At annual fairs at Killorglin, County Kerry, at Ballinasloe in County Galway and at the Killarney and Galway races the tinkers often act as horsedealers or go-betweens. They are known for their ability to 'paint up' or doctor horses; also as 'whisperers' who can calm animals; and as quack 'veterinary surgeons.' When a bargain is made, the gold sovereigns, still used, are spat on for luck, there's a hand-shake and slap, followed by a trip to the pub where the tinker is paid 'boot money.'

It is during the fairs however, that feuds are perpetuated. Hostilities are initiated according to a set pattern. The aggressor lays his hand on a Bible and chants truths about the indiscretions of a member of his family or a member of another clan. Witnesses are called and asked to 'swear on it.' The brawling can go on for weeks until a boxing match between the original contestants is called for and settled by a clan elder or matchmaker.

117

The barrel-shaped caravan is reserved for sleeping in. It is kept scrupulously clean and neat — unlike the tent which is often squalid.

The Poles

Old farming methods die
slowly. At harvest time
there are still Polish
farmers who wield the
traditional long scythes.

SCALE
| 0 | 125 | 250 km |
| 0 | 200 | 400 Miles |

Poland - Present day

Poland - 1919

Poland - 1815

Poland - 1772

Geography and history have not treated the Poles kindly. Though of Slavic origin, they have inhabited lands close to western Europe, close enough to separate them culturally from Russia, the main Slavic nation. For centuries Poles and Russians have fought one another, taking it in turns to gain the upper hand and occupy the other's territory. By rejecting Orthodoxy in favor of the Roman Catholic religion, the Poles became accustomed to the Latin language, and they later forged cultural links with France and Italy. By the 17th century they had an elected monarchy and a parliament of nobles – a liberal system by the standards of those days and one far removed from the despotism of 119

Poland has expanded, contracted and at times vanished between bigger neighbors. Today's Poland fits ethnic realities.

The Poles

Small farmers like these can carry on privately in communist Poland – but their haymaking machine has been rented from the state.

The state supermarkets of Warsaw and Cracow must compete with unofficial markets trading home grown country produce.

tsarist Russia. While the Russians lived an inward-looking, defensive existence, the Poles were ready to travel the civilized world and to bring home its ideas.

But cold military reality eventually put an end to this promising beginning. The flat Polish lands, protected only in the north by the Baltic and in the south by the Tatra Mountains, were hard to defend against well-disciplined cavalry invading from east or west. The Poles might have been able to fight off the Russians, the Prussians or the Austrians one nation at a time, but not all three at once. In 1772, 1792 and 1795 Poland was partitioned between these powerful neighbors and eventually devoured as a nation. Restored to independence in 1918 through a historical quirk – the military defeat of two of the occupying powers and revolutionary chaos in the third – Poland enjoyed 21 precarious years before she again fell victim to a Russian-German conspiracy. In the five years that followed 1939 millions of Poles, about 20 per cent of her population, perished in the indescribable conditions of Nazi extermination camps and Stalinist 'corrective labor'. And this was not all. They had been not only massacred by their traditional enemies, but also betrayed by their British allies. Though

120

(Middle) In southern Poland the steppes give way to wooded mountains where shepherds follow a life far from the rush of the towns.

In Poland the army is versatile. Here on one of the state's collective farms a soldier reaps the harvest.

bound to Poland by treaty, the British did nothing to prevent her military defeat in 1939, and when in 1945 they were called upon with America and Russia to decide Poland's political future, they handed her over to the tender mercies of an unrepresentative government dominated by communists and nominated by Stalin.

It was only by accepting such cruel blows of history that Poland was able in 1945 to embark on another period of nationhood. What Poles had now was a sort of semi-independence, with foreign and defense policies totally under Moscow's control, with some room for manoeuver in strictly internal questions which, while not identical to the Soviet model, were strongly influenced by the imported dogmas of Marx and Lenin. This strange half-existence as an independent country explains many of the complexes which trouble Poles and upset the lives they lead. For them politics are not an élitist hobby to be regarded with detachment and cynicism, but a part of each person's life, recorded in his family history and affecting his very soul. Communism has meant not only strict discipline and sometimes police terror, but also a seemingly irrevocable return to the Russian sphere of influence and a consequent separation from western Europe. Even now, after a quarter of a century of communist rule, there are few Poles, almost certainly less than 10 per cent, who regard this state of affairs with anything but distaste.

None of this means that Poles now lead miserable lives unrelieved by ordinary human joys. A predominantly agricultural country before the war, Poland has now developed a significant industrial base and is slowly raising the living standard of its population. As is only right under socialism, it provides people with the basic essentials of life either free of charge or cheaply. Poles pay nothing for their education or medical treatment. Each family is provided with somewhere to live at a nominal rent. It may be a small flat in a dreary town, but it will at least be cheap, as will be heating and electricity. Problems arise only when a Pole wants to move his flat to a more desirable place like Warsaw or Cracow. Then he will be baffled by the bureaucratic maze, and will have little chance of success unless his reasons for wanting to move are compelling from the state's point of view. The private sector in housing is meager and consequently mercilessly exploits the tenant.

This is but one symptom of a malaise felt by many Poles – the general lack of opportunity for personal economic advancement. Under the constitution every citizen is entitled to a job and a salary, but pay is low by western standards, especially for 'white-collar' jobs, and rises little as one's career progresses. For instance a senior doctor may well receive less than a shipyard worker or miner. A school headmaster will receive less than a taxi-driver and only a little more than a junior schoolteacher. The average monthly salary, about 2,500 zlotys, is equivalent in spending power only to about $60,

so it is hardly surprising that families by and large spend just over half their income on food. Bread is cheap, vegetables are cheap, rent is cheap, but there is little left over for the pleasures of life.

Pay may be low, but hours of work are short. Poles leave their offices at about 3 pm when they return home for the main meal of the day. Public transport within cities is also cheap – less than a penny or a couple of cents for a journey of any length – but it is inadequate, so that people are forced to wait in long queues and then perhaps to travel on the outside running-board of a tram, hanging on to a rail and crushed against other passengers like grapes in a bunch. There are also long queues for food, especially for food of any quality. This is particularly tough on wives who have to do their shopping either before or after work.

One of the main differences between Polish and western society is that a housewife is a rarity in Poland, for almost all married women have regular jobs. In some ways it helps women to lead a fuller life than they would in a country where they are expected merely to run a house and to bring up children. A married woman can plan her own career, organize her working life, and she is not necessarily expected to subordinate her wishes to those of her husband. Women can gain positions of authority in almost any profession: engineering, agriculture or factory management as well as such traditionally feminine areas as medicine and teaching. For this reason Polish women are perhaps a little more self-confident than western women: their life differs little from that of their husbands.

It follows that girls form a higher proportion of university students than is usual in the west. The communist government has achieved its greatest successes in education. Before the war literacy was by no means universal, especially among the peasants, and it was most unusual for a child of peasant origin to enter university. During the war the Nazis and Russians between them killed an estimated 40 per cent of Poland's teachers – part of a common policy of beheading the nation and depriving it of its natural leaders. After the war education was made a high priority and many university places were reserved for young people of working-class or peasant origin.

A Pole's troubles really start when he has left school or university and embarks upon earning a living and raising a family. His education may help him to think and understand about life, but it will not necessarily bring him a decent standard of living. His wife, who may also be well educated, will go out to work not so much to enrich her life or to widen her experience, but simply in order to add another 2,500 zlotys a month to the family income. She and her friends may not like leaving their one-year-old and two-year-old children in state nurseries, prone to an ever-changing succession of child-minders. But there is no getting away from the plain economic fact 121

The Poles

The Polish Empire once reached to the warm Black Sea, but today Poles happily flock to the brisker Baltic spa of Sopot.

of life: a single wage is not enough to support a family.

Theft is commonplace and responsible for vast losses of production. Very little social stigma attaches itself even to those who are caught. 'If you don't steal, you die of hunger' people will cynically comment. They exaggerate, of course, but this is not an uncommon reaction, and it demonstrates a rejection of authority and a disrespect for the law that many people still feel. Other Poles turn away from the state system to work in private enterprise, many types of which are legal in Poland, though not in other communist countries. It is here that large sums of money can still be amassed. A family-run shop, market garden, restaurant or small workshop usually provides a better service than its state-run competitor, and Poles will be ready to pay appropriately. But the communist authorities disapprove of these men, who are the richest in Poland, and they are looked down on by the intellectual élite. It is hard for them to operate, to get their essential supplies, without using bribery to oil the wheels, and often they come to grief. Their premises are raided and closed, and with their associates, they are charged with corruption.

For the peasant's life has changed far less since the war than it has for those in the towns. They still largely farm their own land, working as a family unit rather than as a collective. Their farms are small, so they use horses rather than tractors and own little elaborate machinery. They are religious and pay more attention to the village priest than to the local Party secretary. They are glad to support the church with their money. They live well by Polish standards, since they produce for themselves most of what they need and they endure none of the pressures of urban life. Children seldom leave home, unless they are clever enough to enter university; their labor is needed on the land, part of which they know they will eventually inherit. Of course they have some dealings with the authorities, buying building materials, renting machinery, selling produce, but their lives are not dominated by the state machine.

The most popular leisure activity among Polish men is, without doubt, drinking alcohol. The Slavs have always been great drinkers. Some say this is because of their melancholy disposition. Others say it is the climate that drives them to it. Vodka is cheap (like all 'essentials') and is popularly known as 'the poor man's overcoat'. It is not in the Polish character to drink, or to do anything else for that matter, in moderation. Rather than sip the occasional glass or two the Pole will devote an evening to serious drinking. Alone or with friends, he will visit a succession of 'third category' bars where vodka is served in 100-gram glasses. These large measures he will down in one gulp, if he is a true man, and immediately swallow a glass of water or a chaser – a piece of bread or an egg or salted herring.

If there was a greater chance of recreation, possibly less vodka would be drunk. Football is important, but there are few regular professional teams and most people are not within reach of a ground. Few have cars and public transport is not geared to such events. Sporting activities are encouraged and most Poles will be able through their jobs to join a club that gives them such facilities. The club is all important, since Poles would not usually, as individuals, have the resources to sail, go mountaineering, motorcycle racing, or riding. Anyway the Pole is encouraged to operate as part of a group. The individualist who rebels against this with luck may find some means of achieving what he wants, but there is no doubt that things are made much easier for those prepared to play the game according to the guide-lines laid down by the state.

The poor quality of Polish television means that Poles take a greater interest in theater, cinema, and even in books. They tend either to be cultured or else want to be cultured. Even people with little education are not frightened of poetry or good literature. Polish publishing is of good quality and achieves high sales. Books by almost all of the world's leading writers, alive or dead, are available in Polish translation, and they are bought in

Beneath a Soviet built factory put up after the devastation of World War II a worker's mother visits a sick friend with soup and flowers.

(Top) A priest hears confession in a Warsaw square. Despite the regime's aversion to religion many Poles are fervent Catholics.

(Bottom) Many Poles live in huge overcrowded tenements like this one in Gdansk. Families sometimes live six to a room.

large numbers. It is one way in which Poles can keep in touch with the west, which they look to as the source of their own culture.

Poles live by their emotions. The betrayals and massacres they have recently endured; their low and only very slowly improving standard of living; the apparently endless prospect of dependence upon the Soviet Union; the difficulties the state puts in the way of contact with the west, and with the millions of people of Polish origin who live there – all this would seem a recipe for despair. The fact that Poles so seldom give way to despair is a tribute to their resilience as a nation and, perhaps, to a newly acquired adaptability in the face of the status quo. Traditionally Poles have believed that it is their duty to kick against the pricks: all too often in this century they have lived lives of armed struggle and violence. Their lively temperament and pride as a nation makes it all the more difficult to settle down within the framework, and according to the rules of the socialist camp.

It is only recently that Poles have begun to appreciate that their only hope for happiness is to stop dreaming, make the best of a bad job, and concentrate on what modest improvements are possible in their lot.

123

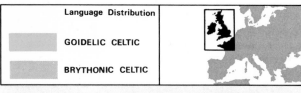

Celtic Fringe
British Isles and Brittany

Language Distribution	
	GOIDELIC CELTIC
	BRYTHONIC CELTIC

GAELIC

Edinburgh

GAELIC

Belfast

Hull

Dublin

WELSH

London

BRETON

Paris

SCALE
0   200   400 km
0   100   200   Miles

In antiquity the Celtic realms covered the whole of the British Isles. Their language, customs and outlook were universal throughout the islands, their art and oral literature venerated everywhere. Except for a number of crosses, intricately worked in stone and bronze, there are few tangible relics of this culture. But among the British people who are distant descendants of the Celts, much of the Celtic mind lives on. There is also a Celtic fringe where people of purer Celtic descent are concentrated and the Celtic influence is profound and enduring. Particularly among Gaelic speaking Irishmen and Scotsmen, and among Cymric speaking Welshmen, the legacy of poetry and song, story-telling and spiritual devotion is found in good measure.

It is in Ireland that the greater part of Celtic literature and tradition survives. Here, in what is essentially a peasant country, in small villages and coastal hamlets,

124

Two Celtic languages survive:
Brythonic, little changed
since 500 BC, and Goidelic,
which came to Ireland from
Spain some centuries later.

The annual Welsh Eisteddfod,
when judges dress as
druids, recalls the Celtic
celebrations when bards and
musicians competed for prizes.

Before an international rugby match, Welsh supporters will readily burst into loud song, including as a rule their Welsh national anthem.

Rugby football for the Welsh is more than a sport – it is a national institution. Top players become popular heroes.

gatherings. Among the older games, hurley is most popular, and horse-racing has lost little of its old appeal.

The Welsh love music, song, dance and games no less than the Irish. In Wales there were similar festivals and gatherings which marked seasons and traditional events. Many of these festivals died out in the seventeenth century, but the Eisteddfod festival, a modern innovation, is more than just a commercial revival. A twelfth century prince once wrote down the rules for his yearly festival in which bards sang or spoke their poems and prizes were given for the best performances in music, choral singing and prose reading. The present-day Eisteddfod recalls these celebrations of ancient times.

Just as the Irish people had their men of learning, the *Filids,* the Welsh had their Druids. The Druids were the source of ancient wisdom – often, it was said, by divine inspiration – and the keepers of their traditions. To Welshmen, Wales was never a land to be scarred by mills, factories and mines (which were to come) but a country of green valleys and song. Their romantic attachment to their past has allowed Cymric, the Welsh Celtic language, to survive despite the encroachments of English people across the mountains. Songs, sagas and legends are all remembered in Cymric. A language so bound up in Welsh history does not die easily.

The Breton people have a saying: 'the Breton peasant fears God and the sea alone.' Bretons too are of Celtic descent. Breton onion-sellers, who seasonally cross the Channel to sell their onions in England and Wales, can understand and be understood by Cymric-speaking Welshmen. But Bretons are more closely related to the Cornish people. It was from Cornwall, in the 5th century, that Celtic people crossed to France where their language and traditions have remained ever since. Both peoples, in more recent history, have been famed for their seafaring exploits; and in their earthiness they both retain much of the ancient Celtic outlook.

For more than two thousand years the Scottish people have defended themselves against invasions from the south and from the sea. Here, old legends tell of past glories; often of ancient victories against the Sassenachs (the Scottish name for Saxons who invaded Britain 1,500 years ago). In the highlands and western islands crofters deny the English influence. These simple farmers live very much in the ways of old Scotland; isolated in small townships or in their crofts, separated by glen and moor, mountain, loch or sea. Ancient stone houses – often circular like those in Ireland – and hilltop forts tell of the agrarian but warlike way of life that once existed throughout Celtic Britain. Here too the Celtic custom of holding tribal or religious assemblies at fixed places is recalled by such occasions as the Highland Games where men gather in various Highland towns for competitive sport (much as the Welsh gather for literary competition). At Lochmaben, in south-west Scotland, the Lochmaben stone reminds the Scots that once their ancestors gathered

local customs hark back to ancient traditions. Pagan rituals involving sympathetic magic linger on, thinly disguised as Christian practices. Child-bearing, for example, was once part of the ritual necessary to bring success in cultivation, and not long ago an ill omen was still attached to unmarried women. Story-telling endures among old men and women who can entertain their families and guests for a year without once repeating the same tale. They spend their evenings reciting stories that might have been told a thousand years before, with voices as vibrant as a Shakespearean actor's – stories sounding as if they were yesterday's news.

The pastoral tradition is strong. Although the Celtic year began on All Hallows Day, November 1st, the other days of importance like St Bridget's Day on February 1st, were also marked with festivals that welcomed the new season. It is by fairs and festivals, not by the calendar, that the countryman dates events. Music, dancing and games played their part in the seasonal

A note on Highland Dress by Sir Iain Moncreiffe, 24th of That Ilk:

After Bonnie Prince Charlie's Rising, the Hanoverian Government proscribed the bagpipes, which have since struck terror into foes as far afield as Tobruk, as 'instruments of war. This man (left) is not a Gurkha, though one of their regiments has bagpipes in Colquhoun tartan (it was raised by a Colquhoun colonel). Nor is he Moroccan, though the Sultan's bodyguard has bagpipes in Maclean tartan because Kaid Sir Harry Maclean organized their band. Nor is he from Udaipur in India where the Maharajah's pipers so moved me by playing 'My Lodging is on the Cold Ground,' which Moll Davies sang before Charles II and which led him to father some of our grandest aristocracy out of her. No, this is a Highland Scotsman.

He is shod in black. (I remember the late Duke of Atholl sent me upstairs to change because I had come down in my kilt wearing brown shoes.) His ankles are protected by white spats to keep out the wet. His stockings are checked and tied with a red garter. In his right stocking is a *sgian dubh* ('black knife,' after the color of its handle.) At one time, the knife was often in the same sheath as a fork.

For long, however, the knife and fork have been kept in the sheath of the dirk or dagger, which he also wears on his right, as it was a left-handed weapon. On his left shoulder is his plaid-brooch to fasten the plaid pleated round his chest and hung down his side. This is the upper part of what was once a huge rug belted round, that kept him warm at night in the heather. The bottom part was cut off in the 18th century and sewn up to form a *Feilidh Beag* or 'little plaid.' We call it a kilt. Its colored checked pattern — known as tartan — once represented the family, regiment or region of its wearer.

Ladies always want to know what is worn beneath. The answer is, nothing. The bit of dead goat in front is his sporran, a Gaelic word meaning 'purse' (the hereditary treasurer of Macdonald of the Isles was called MacSporran). It serves the same functions as a lady's handbag (but rarely includes a powder compact!)

On his head he is wearing a feather bonnet. This is made of ostrich feathers: only chieftains wear eagle's feathers. After the Crimean War battle of the Alma, Lord Raglan promised General Sir Colin Campbell any favor that recognized the Highlanders' bravery. Sir Colin begged 'to wear the Highland feather-bonnet in place of a general's cocked hat.

In his bonnet, our piper is wearing the Red Hackle. This honor is now accorded only to our oldest Highland regiment the Black Watch, though the Fraser Highlanders wore it at the taking of Quebec.

127

The Duke of Atholl's private army of 100 men was given Royal sanction by Queen Victoria in 1844. It is the last private army in Britain.

128

Sword-dancing at the Scottish highland games is performed to the skirl of bagpipes. Arms are raised in imitation of the once-sacred hunted stag.

Scotsmen applaud massive strength at the various highland games each summer. A kilted clansman here puts the shot.

Poteen, a white liquid as potent as whiskey — is distilled from potatoes. Stills must be sited close to a stream — and safely hidden.

A boat draws near a hidden still where *poteen* is stored. Later it will be drunk in the cottages of west coast farmers and fishermen.

In Celtic times *poteen* was drunk at the festivals which marked the seasons for Irish farmers. Now *poteen* is illegal and only drunk secretly.

to worship Maponus, the youthful Celtic God who was patron of both music and markets.

In remote parts of the Hebridean islands the simple kind of farming introduced by the Celts still survives. Sheep, once domesticated by those same early farmers, now run wild. The ancient woollen industry continues among old people, who work on crude looms with heavy yarns. The methods are little changed. The Gaelic oral tradition of literature, although originally Irish, also prevails in Scotland. The stories are different, but they are remembered in the same way. Old men and women lend their broad, lusty voices to the telling of tales that seem to record the whole of the romantic Celtic past. In legends and poems the glory of a fighting nation is not forgotten.

But oral literature can never survive as written works survive. In those realms of elusive culture, generations ago, there was much that will never be known. What hero tales were once recited round the hearth of *broch, crannog* or lowland homestead in Celtic times? How much of their history is lost to the passing generations? What do survive are stone artifacts, legends and the nature of the Scottish people. These things are the heritage of the people, the setting in which a glorious history took place.

What history can tell us, from the pages of Roman and Greek geographers and historians, is that even in Roman times the harbors of Celtic language and culture were shifting. But Celts were not always driven into the west; as the Roman legions pushed westward and northward, many of the Celtic peoples were defeated and absorbed. Some fled to the highlands and islands of the western coasts, and others across the Irish Sea – which has been called the Celtic pond. But also there were others who were hardly touched by the early invasions of Romans or the later incursions of Germanic and Scandinavian peoples. Many Scots, Welsh and Irish people in the mountains and valleys remained largely unaffected.

In the British Isles the Celtic genius, isolated in the western parts, found its fullest expression under the stimulus of Christianity. By the sixth century the Irish were more passionately devoted to their beliefs than any other people in Europe. They became zealous missionaries and monks took to the new art of writing their literature. Many of those ancient manuscripts have been passed down to us – the oldest written work in the British Isles. In Wales also Christianity found firm soil. Today, the chapel is as important a feature of Welsh life as the Druid worship of paganism was before Christianity. Then, as now, the Irish and Welsh Celtic peoples were devout idealists.

The heroic sagas of those people, passed by word of mouth from peasant farmer to his son, or from learned monk to posterity, recall an age of romanticism. In the forests of Ireland, the lochs of the Scottish highlands and the mountains and valleys of Wales the tales were told alongside those of Christian virtue. Few other people have shown so great a tolerance for the heroes and the seers, the magic and the mythology of a heathen past – even when they have been so completely converted to the Christian church.

129

Hurling – played with sticks like hockey sticks – was one of the games played at old Celtic festivals. Today it is popular throughout Ireland.

The Venetians
Italy

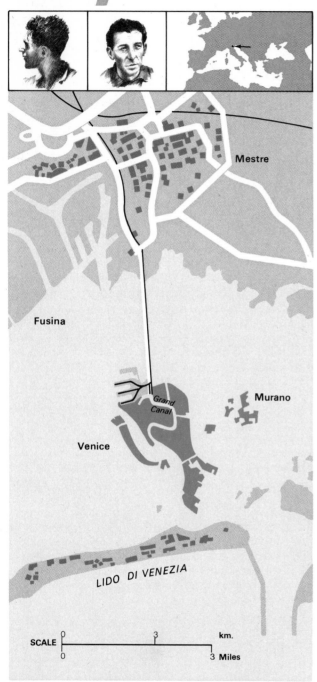

Mestre

Fusina

Grand
Canal

Murano

Venice

LIDO DI VENEZIA

SCALE

	0		3		km.
	0			3	Miles

Venice is cherished in the world's mind as a romantic image or dream. From Shakespeare to Gilbert and Sullivan the world has responded to its name as to a golden and intoxicating vision of gondolas and Doges and the Rialto, of an ancient empire and the gorgeous East held in fee, of St Mark's and the plumed lions: a romantic vision. Some of this romance hopefully became attached to the many other places that borrowed the

name – to 'Little Venice' in London, to the country of Venezuela, to the assorted Venices of Alberta, California, Florida, Louisiana, and Illinois. In the same way, the Italian word for a shore or beach – *lido* – has become a glamor-name for countless places of recreation everywhere, simply because one of the many *lidi* or sandbanks that separate the Venetian lagoon from the Adriatic has become famous as a bathing and sunbathing place for the idle rich, and the beautiful people.

The vision is neither completely false nor completely ignoble. Behind it, the actual Venetians remain: a distinctive and characteristic people, leading their own lives in their own city. To some extent, their life is that of any people in a present-day city of southern Europe: they have television, hospitals, a fine new airport. And it is important to remember that their city exists as an economic, functioning whole, far beyond the limits of what the travel-books call 'Venice' – just as New York extends far beyond the limits of Manhattan.

The old city of Venice is a small island of about 2·7 square miles founded by refugees who fled from invaders during the fifth and sixth centuries to find a safe refuge in that swampy lagoon. At present the largest of the islands which they occupied – the 'Venice' of the guidebooks – has a population of about 175,000; but in 1927 it was incorporated with the other islands of the lagoon and a substantial area of the adjacent mainland into the commune of Venice, an administrative and economic unit of about 120 square miles and a population of over 360,000. Venice in this larger sense is a rapidly-developing, prosperous industrial port, concerned with chemical, metallurgical and other engineering, with the processing of coal, refining of oil and manufacturing of glass and soap, and – as in the days when Venice ruled the seas – with the activity of a naval dockyard.

If this city lives on its past, it does so positively and with an eye to the future. Once the great link and gateway between east and west, Europe's door to the Orient, it is now likely to repeat the pattern and become the principal south-eastern gateway of a newly united Europe.

Although the people of the ancient city on the island are much involved in all this, commuting in both directions along the causeway that links it to the mainland the old island city remains a distinct and separate place, the home of the distinctive people we think of as 'the Venetians'.

It is a weak city, and in two ways. It is weak physically: built upon countless wooden stakes hammered centuries ago into a shifting sub-soil, it is slowly sinking, while – by an unrelated process – the sea itself is rising. The city lives upon, and sometimes beyond, the brink of serious flooding: unless expensive steps are taken its days are numbered.

Then, it is weak economically. The profitable industry is on the mainland – notably in the towns of Mestre and Porto Marghera – and to some extent the island lives

upon the profits. But it depends crucially on the tourist trade – which is heavy in summer – and on two ancillary industries. Venetian glass is one of them. Ornamental glass has been made in Venice since early times. In the Middle Ages the glassworks were banned from the city because of fire-risk and established on the nearby island of Murano. These have recently been revived and as well as a source of income are a considerable tourist attraction. On the island of Burano further north flourishes the similarly traditional art of lace-making. The economy of the city is further helped by the labors of its fishermen and by the temporary or permanent residence of wealthy people who make their money elsewhere and choose to spend it in Venice.

But still the city largely depends on the tourists, who come in their thousands, but will not continue to do so if commercial exploitation makes Venice a less distinctive,

attractive place. The economy of a tourist-attraction can prove self-destructive.

Ethnically, linguistically and by their history and geography the Venetians are a remarkable people. They have been Italian citizens since 1866 and their city contains many from other parts of the country and from further afield. The characteristic appearance of the true-born Venetian is the inheritance of past travels and trading and of Slav, Austrian and even oriental elements in his blood. His nose is large, he tends to be pale and bow-legged. He walks in a way of his own, possibly because circumstances forever compel him to climb over steep bridges. He tends to be reserved, a shade melancholy and distant, governed by a sense of special identity and ancient pride. He has an aloofness from the rest of the modern world.

His speech is distinctive too: 'a sweet bastard Latin' 131

When it rains in Venice, the ladies gather to drink tea in Renaissance-style tea-rooms — built in the late 19th century.

Byron called it. It is often incomprehensible to those who understand ordinary Italian. It is complicated by French, German and Arabic elements, and uttered in a slurred sing-song within which single words seem to disappear. These contractions are faithfully reproduced when the Venetian speech is written. This means, for one thing, that the street-signs of the city baffle unless you have special knowledge. It is not in fact the Italian language: indeed there are several Italian-Venetian dictionaries.

Any seaport town will have its foreign minorities: Venice especially, with its long history of east-west trade. There is a thousand-strong, not fully assimilated, colony of Jews. Many of them still live in the old Ghetto, where two of the five old synagogues are still in use. They have had a mixed past. In the Middle Ages they received a kind of protection from the city, but were treated with suspicion and given inferior status, as is reflected in *The Merchant of Venice*. They still have a strong sense of community. Some are rich; many have middle-class or professional status. Then there are about fifty Greeks, the small remnant of a colony formerly ten thousand strong. They share an Orthodox church with a few Russian residents. There is a handful of Armenians and a few Germans, reminders of an old commercial connection between Venice and Germany. A few Englishmen have their Anglican and very English church, and there are some Americans.

All the same the Venetians are a homogeneous people, with a strong sense of identity and citizenship. In the great days of the Venetian republic, they were ruled, somewhat paradoxically, by an oligarchy that was both harsh and gentle, aristocratic and egalitarian. The old patrician families have passed away. The wealthy and influential groups of present-day Venice are a mixed crowd. Some are of Venetian origin but of mercantile rather than noble greatness. Others have moved in from other parts of Italy. Venice still contains a great deal of money-power, the consequent social ostentation made less vulgar by the old palaces, the gilded private gondolas and the liveried oarsmen.

Despite all this continuing wealth and splendor, there are still slums and squalors. Overall it is a dirty city. Household rubbish is regularly thrown out of windows down into the alleys, or even, despite strict laws against it, into a canal: sewage is discharged directly from each house into the water, then rather inefficiently dispersed by the limited tides of this inland sea. Venice is smelly. The air itself, particularly in winter, is dirty – not only because of industrial pollution from Mestre or Porto Marghera. This is a coal-burning city, and its chimneys – though wonderfully picturesque – are inefficient and hard to sweep, and soot falls steadily.

Venice has little extreme poverty. Political passions are mild, soothed and kept gentle, even among Communists, by the prevailing sense of identity and cohesion, citizen-

ship and equality, to such an extent that some say the

Before the damp winter begins the gondolas of Venice must be overhauled. Woods must be stripped, recarved and then carefully repolished.

Scientists say that Venice is sinking back into the sea. Fortunately ever-watchful photographers are on hand to record the tragedy.

Venetians are an unnecessarily docile people. Like many Italians, they certainly take kindly to domestic service as a life's work. They are, of course, Roman Catholics – at least in the negative sense of not being Protestants. Although their whole environment is charged with the memory of a deeply religious past, here as elsewhere, religious faith seems on the decline. Still, the presence of the Church is formidable. The Patriarch of Venice, who takes precedence over a mere Cardinal or Archbishop, is a major figure in the city, but there is no clericalist rule. The great services in St Mark's tend to be attended by tourists rather than Venetians. Even in their earlier, greater days, these people were Catholics with a difference, riding lightly and sometimes rebelliously upon the authority of Rome, and sometimes finding it possible – given a suitable profit-motive – to ally themselves with Muslim powers against their fellow-Christians.

With little serious crime and hardly any real violence the Venetians have a certain tendency to quiet discreet amorality. There is much petty theft and pilferage, often at the tourists' expense. There is much elaborate padlocking of doors. In the business of daily life, the Venetians practise a sharpness that often comes close to sharp practice. Even in the most romantic episodes of their colorful past, there constantly recurs a note of astute and even shady commercialism. Today every small transaction is likely to include an element of mild duplicity, directed at the tax-inspector or the accountant or at some third party who expects to get a rake-off.

The old commercial empire of Venice has gone, but its people are still businessmen of the sharpest and most hard-headed kind, skilled at driving a hard bargain but honorably keeping their own side of the contract. The capitalist spirit, supported by a tradition of sound public administration, and of integrity and dedication of doctors, lawyers and engineers, thrives in Venice. The system here is different from the corrupt, inefficient bureaucracy of Italy generally, chiefly because the professional men of Venice inherit the tradition of the old Venetian aristocracy.

Things were different in the late eighteenth century, during the decline of the Republic. Then Venice was notorious for dissolute, colorful wildness. But while a certain amount of drunken jollity still echoes down the canals and alleys at midnight, and the international smart set behave in Venice as they do elsewhere, the Venetians themselves are a modest, moral people, especially in sexual matters. Prostitution has nearly been stamped out. In Venice the free-and-easy ways of permissiveness of many western cities are practically unknown. A young Venetian girl will still take it for granted that her destiny and fulfilment are to be found within marriage. She will understand that to safeguard this destiny, her liberty will be curtailed. Only exceptionally will she go out alone with a young man, unless they are engaged. But young Venetians frequently are engaged: Venice seems full of happy lovers, looking forward to the day when they will be carried off to church by gondola, the bride's veil streaming, the bridegroom awkward in formal clothes.

In this city of family life and large patriarchal families marriage is important. Children are adored. They are dressed with immense and admiring care. Their fathers carry and cherish and cuddle them in public, to a degree which might be considered unmanly in some countries. Even so, the Venetian child is not altogether fortunate. There are few playgrounds, only one park, too far for many to reach. There are only the endlessly intricate squares and alleyways to play in. Educationally the schools are good, but their buildings are dark, old-fashioned and rather grim, with neither playing-fields nor yards, and the children are pressed hard. Their parents expect them to work, and to get on. They seem to grow up quickly.

Like children anywhere, they find their opportunities around the canals and the mudflats, roller-skating and scuffling between gangs. As you go down the social scale into the poorer quarters, you find the children are more relaxed, cheerful and scruffy. When death comes eventually in this waterborne city a funeral takes on a distinctively gloomy and poetic sort of beauty. Napoleon appointed the island of San Michele the city's cemetery. There the coffin is taken, in a funeral boat little more than a gondola if the family is poor, but in a large motor-boat, ornamented and richly draped, if they are rich. The dignity of the occasion may be somewhat marred if several funeral parties reach San Michele at the same time: there may be jockeying for position, an unseemly element of racing. The cemetery itself is spacious and peaceful, cluttered with monuments and mausoleums of every conceivable design, interspersed with flower-beds. It is always thronged with visitors. Despite the beauty of the city, there is a melancholy in the Venetian air, which seems to encourage a brooding sadness, a preoccupation with death and the macabre. 133

The Europeans

Many of the peoples of Europe at the time of Christ, from the Gauls to the Anatolians, were dominated by the Roman Empire. On its fringes the Germanic, Nordic and Slavic peoples were soon to extend their frontiers and change the shape of Europe; but the Celts in Britain and Danubians in eastern Europe were to be submerged.

As the Roman Empire declined, the Goth and Vandal migrations and raids took Nordic Scandinavian people to most parts of Europe. In the centuries up to 500 AD, Scandinavians settled as far afield as Britain, North Africa and the Baltic.

Roman decline permitted the expansion of Slavic peoples from the Russian steppe, westward into Europe as far as Germany. Warlike Huns, originally a central Asiatic people, settled in Balkan lands and attempted to conquer both Italy and Germany.

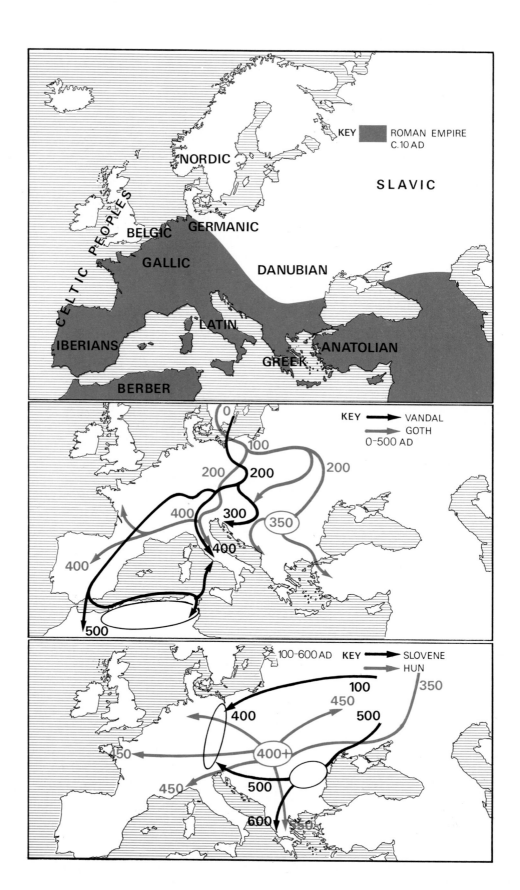

KEY — ROMAN EMPIRE C.10 AD

NORDIC
SLAVIC
CELTIC PEOPLES
BELGIC
GERMANIC
GALLIC
DANUBIAN
IBERIANS
LATIN
ANATOLIAN
GREEK
BERBER

KEY — VANDAL — GOTH 0-500 AD

KEY — SLOVENE — HUN 100-600 AD

their migrations during The First Millennium AD

The 5th and 6th centuries saw the height of the German Folkwandering period. Saxons raided and settled in much of England and also in parts of central Europe. The Franks expanded into Gaul, established several kingdoms and raided as far south as Spain and Italy.

The Danes were frequent raiders and settlers on the coastlands of western Europe in the 9th and 10th centuries. In Britain they mingled with Saxon and Celtic people; in France they settled in Normandy — from where their descendants launched their conquest of England.

The Bulgars settled in Balkan lands and around the Baltic, giving their name to Bulgaria. Ugars, from the Urals, speaking a non-Indo-European tongue, came to settle both in Finland and Hungary. The Arab empire stretched across north Africa into Spain; the Turkish, across much of south-eastern Europe.

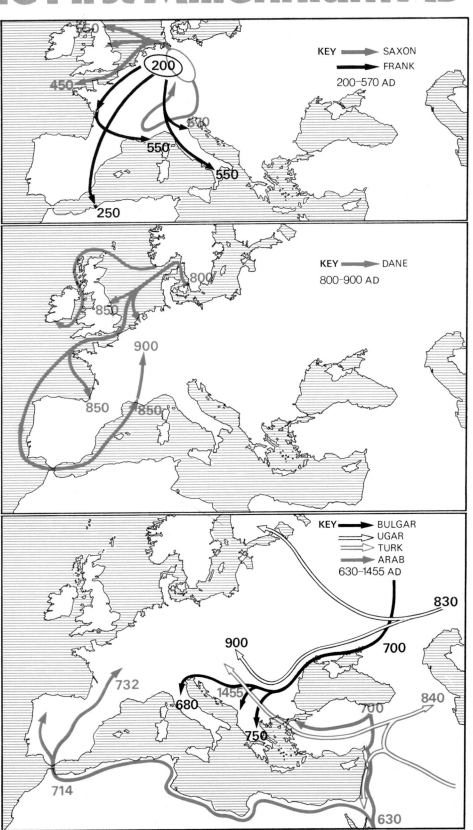

KEY — SAXON
— FRANK
200–570 AD

KEY — DANE
800–900 AD

KEY — BULGAR
— UGAR
— TURK
— ARAB
630–1455 AD

135

Glossary
Europe

IBERIAN PENINSULA

Portuguese   Gibraltarian   Catalan   Andalusian

The ancient neolithic Iberian people has been ethnically and culturally interwoven with people from many parts of Europe – Celts, Scandinavians, Greeks, Romans, Arabs, Berbers and Jews – to produce the modern Spaniard and Portuguese. The Romans described the Iberians as a diminutive, wiry people with dark skins and small faces – the traditional Mediterranean type. But long before the Romans came, in the last millenium BC, Celtic tribes had breached the mountain passes of the Pyrenees. The withdrawal of the Roman armies was followed by further invasions from the north: Goths and Vandals, Cimbrians from Denmark and Suevians from Sweden. They swept through Spain driving bands of Alans from the Russian steppe before them.

Vandals gave their name to Andalusia (Vandalusia), Goths to Catalonia (Gothlandia) and the Suevians to such villages as Suevos. Those who settled were assimilated. In the 8th century the Moors invaded across the Straits of Gibraltar. Their invasion was to leave an indelible mark; as persistent as the name given to Gibraltar (in Arabic: *Jebel Tarik* or Rock of Tarik, after the Arab governor of Tangier). The Moorish hordes overran Spain and Portugal; the Berber rank and file settled in the central mountainous parts most like their homeland, while their Arab leaders concentrated in the cities which soon became centers of Islamic culture. The Moorish occupation lasted almost 500 years. Many Christian crusades were sent against them; and with the Inquisition in the 15th century the remaining Arabs and Jews were finally expelled.

The **Andalusians** live in the south of Spain. They had some of the earliest contacts with Mediterranean traders like the Cretans and the Phoenicians during the last two millenia BC. Cadiz was originally Gadir, a Phoenician colony. The brief conquest by the Vandals from Scandinavia had a profound genetic influence and also gave the region its name – but it was the 500 years of Moorish occupation which was to give modern Andalusians much of their mongrel blood. Today the old Andalusian nobility contrasts with the simple peasants, who seem almost Arabic in appearance. Andalusia is the home of classical bull-fighting and much else that is regarded as traditionally Spanish.

The **Basques** live on the coast and in the Pyrenees near the south-east corner of the Bay of Biscay, in both Spain and France. They have a distinctive language unrelated to any of the other European languages. Physically, the Basques more closely resemble some ancient, pre-historic people than any other living Europeans – largely because of their isolation by the Pyrenees mountains. Many of their ancient customs, ceremonies and games still prevail.

The **Catalans** live in north-eastern Spain. They were among the first people to be conquered by the Romans, and were later overrun by Alans, Goths and Moors. The Catalan language, which has a Latin origin, was preserved throughout this time of successive invasions. After the Christian reconquest of Spain, the Catalan language became more widespread and today survives in Catalonia and as far south as Valencia.

The **Castilians** who live in northern and central Spain preserve much of their historic cultural aristocracy. Castilian is still the literary language of Spain and, with certain differences, of Spanish America. The Castilian people are traditionally noble, adventurous and courageous – and fervent Roman Catholics. During the period of Spanish conquest of the Americas, it was Castilians who commanded and led the armies and ships. Today, with Madrid at their heart, Castilians take pride in their history – their grandiose architecture, their attachment to the established church and to political authority.

The **Gibraltarians** live on the Rock of Gibraltar and are descended from Moorish, Spanish, Italian and Maltese people. The word comes from the Arabic name given to the Rock in the eighth century – Jebel Tarik, or Rock of Tarik – when the Moors began their conquest of Spain. Gibraltar's position at the western entrance to the Mediterranean has always made it an important strategic stronghold; in Greek times it was known as one of the Pillars of Hercules. Since the 18th century it has been a British possession and Gibraltarians have spoken English and resisted absorption into Spain.

The **Portuguese**, like all the people of the Iberian peninsula, are of mixed descent. Celts, Romans, Scandinavians, Berbers and Arabs have all contributed to their ethnic make-up and culture. Their language, however, is evolved from the Latin of the Roman invaders of almost 2,000 years ago. It was not until the 12th century that Portugal became an independent kingdom, at a time when most of the Arab and Berber people had been expelled. Today the Portuguese are proud of 700 years of nationhood. Roman Catholicism still dominates much of their life – and they remain in control of several old colonies.

The **Sephardic Jews** prospered in Spain during the Middle Ages. They excelled as lawyers and scholars. During the Inquisition in the 15th century they were expelled. Some returned to the Middle East. Others went to the Balkans where some still speak *Ladino*, a Spanish-Hebrew language. Many more went to Holland and England where their descendants prosper.

Sicilian   Southern Italian   Savoyard   Maltese

ITALY AND THE MEDITERRANEAN ISLANDS

The Italian people are related to many other Mediterranean peoples – the early Greeks, Hebrews, Etruscans, Asiatic Avars and Magyars, the later Byzantine Greeks and North African Moors – as well as to people from central, eastern and northern Europe, the Celts and the Scandinavians. The first trading expeditions to visit Italy were those of the Mycenaeans (early Greeks) at about 1,500 BC who traded throughout the Mediterranean by the routes followed later by Phoenician and Greek seafarers. The Etruscans arrived from Asia Minor in the 8th century BC and settled in Tuscany. During the 5th century BC Celts brought their Iron Age culture and about this time Greeks made settlements in southern Italy and Sicily. But soon the Roman expansion began. The city of Rome was named after the Ruma, one of the Etruscan clans.

Etruscans were defeated and their language overwhelmed by Latin. Across Italy the people were steadily Romanized, but everywhere the Romans were a separate, conquering minority who imposed only their organisation and their culture; other distinct Italian types remained. From the Imperial provinces people of other nationalities came as slaves, traders, and mercenaries. When the Roman Empire crumbled in the 5th century there were renewed invasions from the north by Gothonic people, later followed by influxes of Moors, Byzantine Greeks, and Asiatic peoples who took advantage of Italy's fragmented city states. Among Italians of today, long united in language, there still exists a great variety of physical types which recalls their mongrel ancestry.

The **Balearic Islanders** are closely akin to the Catalan people of Spain – but the long period of Roman occupation left its mark on both the islanders and their culture. Romans were succeeded by invasions of Vandals, Moslems and medieval Normans. Today while the majority speak Catalan, a small élite speak Castilian.

The **Corsicans** live in an island north of Sardinia which relies economically on olives and wine. The Ligurians from north-west Italy came 2,000 years ago, followed by Phocaeans from central Greece, Romans, Vandals and Goths. Since 1815 Corsica has been French. Every Corsican proudly knows that Napoleon was born here.

The **Cypriots** live on the third largest island in the Mediterranean. Racially 80% are Greek with a minority of Turks. There has rarely been peace between the two groups.

The **Maltese** live on a group of islands between Europe and Africa in the central channel that connects the east and west basins of the Mediterranean Sea. The Maltese, originally central European immigrants in the Late Stone Age, have been mixed with successive colonizing peoples: the Phoenicians (from what is now the Lebanon), Greeks, Romans, and to a small extent,

British. Even today the great powers envy Malta's strategic position. The Maltese speak both English and Phoenician Maltese (a language akin to Syriac and Arabic).

The **Oscans** are descended from people of southern Italy who spoke the long-extinct Campanian dialect imposed on them by Samnite invaders in 500 BC. The Oscan, Volscian and Umbrian languages formed, with Latin, one of the two groups of Italic languages. The last known Oscan inscription was written just before the eruption of Vesuvius in 79 AD. Oscans now speak Italian and live in Calabria, Puglia, Lucania and Campania, the area round Naples.

The **Romans**, the ancient conquerors of much of Europe were descended from central Europeans, who came down the Italian peninsula around 1,000 BC, and from Etruscans who originated in Asia Minor, settled in north Italy around present-day Florence and migrated south to the plains of Latium (from which the Romans' Indo-European language, Latin, takes its name). Despite the collapse of the Roman Empire in the 5th century AD, the Romans assimilated the Goths, Vandals and Huns who swept down from central Europe. The present population of the city of Rome is drawn from all parts of Italy.

The **Sardinians** are of similar stock to the Italians and live in an island separated from Corsica in the north by a narrow strait. They have been colonized by Greeks, Romans, Saracens from north Africa, and Aragonese from Spain. The island passed from Austrian to Piedmontese (later Italian) hands in 1848.

The **Savoyards**. Savoy is a mountainous region in both France and Italy. In the 5th century the Savoyards were conquered by Burgundians, then by Franks. They have been ruled by Charlemagne, Germans and the Holy Roman Empire. The Royal House of Savoy unified all Italy in the last century. The Savoyards speak Italian and French.

The **Sicilians** live on the largest island of the Mediterranean divided by a narrow strait from mainland Italy, and 90 miles from the African coast. Sicilians are mixed in stock, since they have been colonized by a variety of people. The Phoenicians, originally from the Lebanon, invaded from their colony of Carthage (modern Tunis) in 500 BC; then came the Greeks followed by Romans, Byzantines, Arabs, Normans. The people of this poor island are small and dark. They speak Italian. The world's most successful criminal organization – the Mafia – originated in Sicily.

137

Ukranian   Tatar   Muscovite   Pole

EASTERN EUROPE

The Slavic and Baltic speaking peoples of eastern Europe extend from as far north as Latvia and northern Russia, to Bulgaria in the south. Until the Middle Ages Lithuania and Latvia were among the most isolated parts of Europe, hemmed in by great swamps and forests. They retained much of their pagan culture. The Baltic language (often thought as close to the proto-Indo-European tongue of 5,000 years ago as Sanskrit) at that time embraced much of western Russia – and was only displaced and reduced by the encroachments of Gothones, Slavs, Finno-Ugrians and Germans.

Poland, from *pol* the Slavic word for plain, was a kind of funnel through which peoples from Russia and central Asia migrated into Germany, Denmark and the Low Countries. Before this expansion, much of Russia west of the Urals had been occupied by Finno-Ugrian speaking peoples, who were mostly submerged beneath the following Slavic tide. Russia – from the Finno-Ugrian word, *Ruotsi,* for the invading Scandinavians in the 8th century – is the cradle of the Slavic peoples. Until early Christian times other migrations, of Goths, Huns and Avars, passed them by – and then they spread out in all directions; westward into Poland, south and east into other parts of Russia.

For Russia, later incursions by Mongol and Tatar peoples from central Asia during the early Middle Ages, were to have a profound effect. But in central Europe these did not reach far. Czechoslovakia is a wedge of Slavic-speaking people in German-speaking central Europe.

The **Ashkenazim** were the northern group of Jews who settled along the Rhine. In the 11th century the Crusaders persecuted them and they moved east. Most settled in Russia and Poland. Forbidden to own land, they became dealers in jewels and precious metals and lived in ghettoes in the cities. They still speak Yiddish, a form of medieval German enriched by Hebrew and Slavic words. They were almost always persecuted – in Russia they suffered *pogroms,* meaning 'assaults' in Russian. In World War II the Nazis exterminated 5 to 7 million of them and many of the refugees and survivors went to the USA.

The **Cossacks** were not an ethnic group but were Slav families who lived on the Russian frontiers and gave military service to the Russian Empire. Each man fought for Russia from the age of 18 to 38. The word Cossack may come from the Turkic *qssak* – 'adventurer'. There are now 11 scattered Cossack groups from Amur on the Chinese border, to Kuban and Terek in the north Caucasus, Astrakhan on the Caspian Sea, and the Urals in the west.

The **Czechs** are a Slav people who, by the 10th century, controlled Bohemia in central Europe. Most became Roman Catholics. Today they predominate in the state of Czechoslovakia.

The **Estonians**, one of the Finnish tribes who originated near the Ural Mountains, live in the northernmost of the Baltic states. In 1219 the conqueror Waldemar subdued the war-like Estonians and sold the country to the Knights of the Sword (German crusaders). The Estonians became serfs. Rarely left in peace, at the end of World War II their country was incorporated in the USSR.

The **Latvians**, or Letts, were until the 10th century of the same group as the Lithuanians. They live on the Baltic coast between Estonia to the north and Lithuania to the south. They became Lutheran while Lithuania stayed Roman Catholic. Fair and blue-eyed they are like the Lithuanians in looks as well as in language.

The **Lithuanians** speak the oldest surviving Indo-European language, a Baltic dialect similar to the ancient Sanskrit of India. Their empire once stretched from the Baltic to the Black Sea. From 1385 they were dominated by Poland, and later by Russia. Their country was independent between the two world wars but is now part of the USSR. Many are still Roman Catholics.

The **Mordvins** number nearly 2 million. Many now live in their own region of the USSR. They speak two dialects of a Finno-Ugric language: Erzya and Moksha, and preserve many of their old customs and beliefs.

The **Poles** are a Slav people who built a great empire in the 14th century by combining with the Lithuanians and defeating the Ruthenians centered on Kiev. The Polish empire, which once stretched from the Baltic to the Black Sea, was partitioned between Austria, Prussia and Russia. Many of the Poles are still fervent Roman Catholics – and fiercely proud of their Polish identity.

The **Russians** are descended from the Slav forest tribes, overrun in the 9th century by Hungarian and Turkish nomads. The Rus, a northern tribe led by a Swede named Rurik, were perhaps invited to end the troubles. With Kiev and Moscow as their centers, the Russians gradually and doggedly pushed their frontiers out in all directions – vainly seeking the security of natural frontiers which steppe people never have.

The **Slavs** are the largest linguistic group in Europe. They include Russians, Poles, Czechs, Slovenes, Slovaks, Bulgars, Serbs and Croats. In the 1st century AD they migrated from the Danube Basin. Some went west, where they were known as Wends. Others went south, and reached the Balkans in the 5th century. Others went east, colonized Siberia and reached as far as the Pacific and Alaska.

Czechs by Moravia, but linguistically and culturally they are close to the Czechs. The Slovaks have

Irishman   Scotsman   Cornishman   Welshman

been peasants in the same part of central Europe since the 5th century. Today almost all live in the eastern part of Czechoslovakia, but some live in Hungary.

The **Tatars** in the 5th century were Mongols who swept south and west from the Gobi Desert, build-ing a huge empire under Genghis Khan and others. By admixture they have now become more Ural-Turkish than Mongol with sharp straight noses, round wide eyes and white skin. In Europe they are represented by Kazan Tatars on the Volga River, Nogai Tatars in the Crimea, and Bashkirs in the Urals.

The **Ukrainians** live in the vast steppes, snow-bound in winter, of the Ukraine Republic. The 3rd largest republic in the USSR, the Ukraine contains 20% of the Soviet population. Known sometimes as Little Russians, they speak a Russian dialect. Their capital, Kiev was the capital of old Russia.

THE BRITISH ISLES

Far from being isolated, the British Isles have drawn settlers from every part of Europe – Celts and Ibero-Celts; Scandinavians and Germanic people; Romans, early Greek traders and Normans; and, in more recent times, migrants from the farthest corners of the world. Of all Europeans the British are perhaps the most ethnically composite.

By the time of the Roman invasion almost all inhabitants of the islands were Celtic speaking. The Picts in northern Scotland were the first people to be called Britons, but they were later overwhelmed by Scots from northern Ireland. As Roman power weakened the gates were opened to Gothonic invaders from Germany and the Low Countries. Angles, Saxons and Jutes established themselves on the coastlands of southern and eastern England. Norsemen settled in the northern parts, in Scotland and Ireland. The invaders pressed inland and Romanized Celts were Anglicized – Anglo-Saxon became the common language throughout England. The arrival of the Normans brought a fresh cultural sophistication and led to the unification of England.

Among isolated people of the highlands, in Wales and parts of Scotland and Ireland, the cultural and linguistic intermingling was less profound. Celtic language and traditions were preserved, while elsewhere they were sub-merged. But also regional differences of custom and outlook remain, legacies of each of the invading peoples. It is too early to predict whether the recent influxes of Indians, Africans and West Indians will be as well absorbed.

The **Cornish** people stand out from their English neighbors. They are closely related to the Welsh Celtic people and until recent times were famous seafarers and retained their own language. In the 6th century many Cornishmen migrated to Brittany to escape the Saxons. The isolation of Cornwall beyond its moorlands has enabled the Cornish to preserve many of their old Celtic characteristics.

The **English** predominate among peoples of the British Isles. Ethnically the most composite, their characteristics are drawn from Celts, Romans, Germanic, Norse and Norman peoples. In language English is a predominantly Anglo-Saxon tongue. They are noted for their phlegm and a certain humor in adversity, but perhaps take most pride in their sense of fair play.

The **Irish** Celtic literature survives as the oldest written work in Britain – and this despite the incursions of Vikings, Saxons and Normans on the soil of old Ireland. Irish Gaelic, or Erse, now assiduously promoted by the government, has survived particularly along the thinly populated west coast. Many of the Irish are as dark as the Celtic Welsh; there are also many who are tall, fair and blue-eyed. Yet the cultures of invading Danes, Normans and English have been imbued with much that is Celtic; not least a vigorous imagination and a sense of the other world.

The **Manx**. The first inhabitants of the Isle of Man in the Irish Sea were Celts who arrived in 200 BC. A thousand years later the island was settled by Norsemen. These Norse and later English settlers adopted local customs and language. Until less than a hundred years ago the Celtic Manx tongue survived. Although part of the United Kingdom, the people have their own laws and legislature.

The **Scots**, since the Roman invasion of Britain 2,000 years ago have fiercely resisted invaders. Ferocity and the natural barriers of their lochs and highlands have helped to preserve an individuality characterized today by grit, dourness and canni-ness. Scots Gaelic (a branch of Irish) was brought to Scotland in the fifth century and soon dis-placed the Brythonic Celtic of the Picts. Vikings established themselves in the Western Isles from the 9th to the 13th centuries. The lowlands have increasingly come under the influence of English neighbors, but Glasgow has been, for a century and a half, a major industrial center in its own right.

The **Welsh**. For 2,000 years Wales has been a refuge for recalcitrant peoples. There Celtic tribes defended themselves against Roman and Saxon invaders, and Welsh, the main branch of Brythonic Celtic, is spoken to this day. They are small, dark, poetic people with a powerful musical tradition and sense of identity.

Walloon   Provençal   Breton   Fleming

FRANCE AND THE LOW COUNTRIES

Centuries of contact and invasions from all parts of Europe – from Celts and Romans, Scandinavians and Germans – have produced the varied peoples of France, Belgium and Holland. In antiquity, however, France was remote from the centers of civilization. Groups of Bronze Age people remained isolated until the Celtic invasions of the last millenium BC which imposed an Iron Age culture and their Indo-European speech. Older languages – like Basque – lingered on, but with the Romans came a form of vulgar Latin which soon replaced the Celtic idioms. The collapse of Rome was followed by invasions by Germanic tribes, and the Franks overran Gaul where Gallo-Latin was to become the basis for modern French. In the 5th century Cornishmen carried a Celtic dialect back to Brittany and a Danish colony was founded in Normandy in the 10th century. Germanic settlements in Alsace and Lorraine were only later incorporated into France. The darker, more Latin people of southern France and Provence testify to the profound Italian influence in these regions.

Many of the migrations across the North Sea to England were launched from the coasts of the Low Countries. In pre-Roman times the people of the Low Countries were Celtic-speaking. During the Roman occupation many Germanic tribes filtered in and were linguistically assimilated. Frisians soon occupied much of Holland and Saxons migrated through the Low Countries; some settled and others continued to England. Modern Dutch and Flemish spring from these Germanic dialects; while in southern Belgium the Walloons speak a dialect of French.

The **Bretons'** history has been largely determined by their isolation from the rest of Europe. The early pre-Celtic people have left huge stone monuments but little else. The early Celtic people of Brittany were Latinized – and only after the Roman decline did other Celts from Cornwall migrate to Brittany. Until then the Bretons had been pagan, but Christianity in Brittany brought by missionaries from Ireland and Britain, dates from the same period as the Celtic colonization. Bretons have never lost their attachment to old Celtic traditions and although shorter and darker than the Cornish, they are much alike in character and temperament.

The **Flemings** live in northern Belgium and Holland and speak a language of Frankish derivation. The Franks were a German tribe who swept across the Low Countries in the early Christian era and overwhelmed the vulgar Latin language left by the Romans. The historic land of Flanders suffered many invasions by French, Germans and Spaniards – but modern Holland and Belgium are among the most liberal, democratic and stable states of Europe.

The people of **Luxembourg** are bounded in the north and west by Belgians, and by Germans in the south and east. The original inhabitants (in Iron Age times) were Belgae or Germanic-Celtic people who were Latinized when the Romans swept across Gaul. Today the people of the Grand Duchy of Luxembourg speak both French and German alongside Letzebursch which is, like Dutch and Flemish, a derivative of the old Frankish tongue.

The **Normans** live in Normandy in north-west France. They are descended from Danish colonists who settled on the coastal regions of Gaul in the 10th century. They adopted French customs and language (a mixture of Frankish and vulgar Latin) and then, like the Folkwandering Scandinavians, conquered England. This was their most successful venture. To England they took a fresh sophistication, a culture evolved from the Danish, Frankish and Latinized French. Many Normans of today have characteristics familiar among Scandinavian people – the blond or red hair, the tall frame. Many old Norse terms for the sea and ships abound in the Norman *patois*.

The **Picards** live in an area of northern France, east of Normandy. In Roman times their land was known as Belgica Secunda and not until the 13th century were the Picards recognized when Charlemagne had his capital at Noyon. Their language was at that time Gallo-Latin and the people were of mixed Celtic-Roman descent. Another movement, of the Flemish people, brought both a fresh cultural impulse and new skills – especially those of weaving for which the Picards have become famous.

The **Provençals** live in the region of southern France first colonized by the Greeks in 600 BC. They founded the trading port of Messalia (now Marseilles). The Roman legions passed through Provence on their rampage through Gaul and the people were Latinized in both language and culture. Much of that Mediterranean influence is visible in the appearance of Provençals today. They are closer to Italians than other Frenchmen. Their language is derived from the old Langue d'Oc – the tongue of the first troubadours.

The **Walloons** live in the south of Belgium, in districts formerly occupied by Romanized Celts, where the Frankish influence was weaker than among the Flemish of the north. They speak a dialect of French (Walloon is a Gothonic word for 'foreigner', similar to the words Welsh and Wallach). Since the Reformation, the Catholicism of the Walloons and the Protestantism of the Flemish has emphasized the cultural and linguistic rift between the two peoples.

Bulgar   Albanian   Rumanian   Magyar

HUNGARY AND THE BALKANS

Balkan lands encompass Latin, Slavic and Greek speaking peoples in a part of Europe which has throughout its history been a highway for intensive migrations. Invaders came in waves across the Hungarian plain: Illyrians, Celts, Germans, Slavs, Mongols, Turks and Ugrians. Not until the 9th century did the Magyars come from the land between the Volga and the Urals to implant their outlandish tongue on the settled Slav, Avar and Gothonic speaking inhabitants. All contributed to the ethnic fabric of modern Hungarians.

Slav-speaking Yugoslavians retain elements of far earlier established peoples. Montenegrans and Bosnians, isolated in the mountains, slowly forsook their native tongues in favor of Serbian, but were otherwise little affected by the Slav encroachments. Albanians are closely related to the tall people of Montenegro; their language preserves much of an ancient Indo-European language (Thraco-Phrygian) which elsewhere is long extinct.

The Rumanians are not lineal descendants of Roman colonists, but do preserve a form of Latin in their language. Following the Roman withdrawal, waves of central Asiatic and Russian peoples drove early inhabitants westward. These returned later and Latin evolved as a language of the patriots.

The physical appearance of Greeks today was probably ancient in Trojan times. Their language had penetrated most of Greece 2,000 years ago, except in islands like Crete, where the Minoan civilization existed 3,000 years BC, and early dialects lingered on.

The **Albanians** call their mountainous homeland on the Adriatic coast south of Yugoslavia 'the country of the eagles'. An unusually tall race, their origins are possibly in a people who spoke the Thraco-Phrygian group of languages who inhabited the Balkans long before the Slav invasions of the 5th century AD. Hardy and nationalistic, most Albanians live in the mountains, rather than the coastal towns and cling to a Muslim heritage.

The **Bosnians** are a mixture of old Illyrian and Slav stock, a small minority in mid-Yugoslavia. Their land was buffeted by Hungary and Croatia in the north and Byzantium and Serbia in the south. When the Turks left Bosnia in 1699, their ancient identity as Slavs re-asserted itself. Sarajevo is today's capital of Bosnia-Herzegovina.

The **Bulgars** are a stocky, dark haired people of sturdy peasant origin. Their mountainous homeland – Bulgaria – is bordered by Turkey, Greece, Rumania and Yugoslavia. They migrated south from the Volga river (whence their name) to present-day Bulgaria in the 4th century. They have stayed staunchly Orthodox Christian, despite the 500 year occupation by the Turks until 1878.

The **Greeks**. From the middle of the second millenium BC Minoans from Crete settled extensively in island and mainland Greece, to mingle with the already settled Mycenaeans and Dorians

from central Europe. Phoenicians (from modern Lebanon), Romans, Celts, Goths, Slavs, Vlachs and Turks have since made their ethnic contribution to the waywardly brilliant people of today.

The **Macedonians'** territory crosses north-west Greece and spills over into Yugoslavia. In the towns the people tend to be of Greek stock while the peasants are mostly Bulgars – Slav people originally from the Volga River. There is also some Vlach and Turkish blood due to numerous Turkish invasions. Although many are Muslims most are Greek Orthodox Christians.

The **Magyars** are Finno-Ugric peoples who spread first from the Urals of Central Asia to the Carpathian Mountains. They migrated from there in the 9th century and settled in Hungary. They are related – most noticeably today by linguistic affinity – to the Finns, whose westward migration from the Urals carried them north. The lively, imaginative Magyars are the dominant ethnic group of Hungary and are traditionally Roman Catholic.

The **Montenegrans**. The name of this tough, self-reliant people means 'people of the Black Mountains', a range which forms the Adriatic seaboard of south-west Yugoslavia. Serbian fugitives from Turkish rule built up a mountain stronghold around Zeta. Together with the hill

people of Herzegovina they fended off Venetians as well as Turks. Anyone showing fear was dressed as a woman and driven out.

The **Rumanians** today are mostly Vlachs – also known as Wallachs – a Slav people often thought to be of Latin descent. Pockets of Rumanians live in North Greece (where they are called 'Kutzo'), Serbia, and Bulgaria. Their language is close to Latin – a legacy of the Romans.

The **Serbo-Croats** live in northern Yugoslavia. The Serbs' sole distinction from the Croats is religious – and therefore cultural. These southern Slavs were divided between Byzantium (Istanbul) and Rome, leaving the Serbs today Eastern Orthodox (using the Cyrillic script) and the Croats Roman Catholic. The Serbo-Croats reached their present homeland from the Dniester basin in the 6th century. Serbs form 42%, Croats 22% of Yugoslavia's population.

The **Slovenes** reached their homeland – centered on the Yugoslav coastal town of Ljubljana – after migrating from the Dnieper headwaters somewhat later than their closest ethnic relatives, the Serbo-Croats. The Slovenes spill over into Austria and Italy. Their language, culture and stock is Slav and close to the Serbo-Croats. Slovenes are Roman Catholic, and form 5% of Yugoslavia's population.

141

Frisian

Alsatian

Bavarian

Prussian

GERMANY, SWITZERLAND AND AUSTRIA

Descendants of Danubians, Celts, Scandinavians, Germanic and Slavic people are all found in this part of central Europe. From 500 BC the Celtic people spilled out to all parts of Europe from their homeland in south-western Germany. The Celts spread their Iron Age culture passed to them by Danubians from Halstatt, in Austria. With the arrival of Gothonic people from Scandinavia, the Folk-wandering (later to carry Angles, Saxons and Jutes to England) of the Germanic tribes began. In the early Christian era, partly as a defense against Roman encroachments, German tribes grouped together into larger confederations. During the 3rd and 4th centuries Slavs penetrated along rivers and the Baltic coast from the east, into Germany. But later, through the Middle Ages, the Germans vigorously expanded. At the expense of both Slavic and Baltic settlements, Germans established themselves as far as Poland, Hungary and Russia.

In Switzerland the mountain valleys were ideal conditions in which ancient Alpine peoples could survive. But Celts penetrated from the north and by Roman times the Helvetii, a Celtic-speaking Swiss tribe, were reputedly the bravest in Gaul. By the 9th century Germanic idioms had been implanted in all but the southern and eastern parts where a vulgar Latin (now French and Italian) had already taken root. In Austria too the Celts had overwhelmed the original Danubian people during the late Iron Age. During the 6th and 7th centuries Germanic people implanted their language, though Slavs from across the Hungarian plain also left many Slavic idioms.

The **Alsatians** live in a region on the borders of France and Germany which has been in dispute between the two countries since Roman times. At the time of Charlemagne the Alsatians were at the heart of the Frankish Empire. Although Alsace is now in France, the people still speak a dialect of German.

The **Austrians'** ancestors were Celts, Danubians – ancient slash-and-burn agriculturalists – and Romans; Asiatic Huns and Avars who drove the Slavic people before them; and more recently Germans and Scandinavians. Austria is a natural highway between Slavonic and Germanic peoples. Tall north European types mingle with short, sturdy Alpine people and stocky east-Baltic types often found in Hungary. Today almost all Austrians are German speaking; but proudly distinguish their own ethnic, historical and rich cultural heritage, associated above all with Hapsburg power.

The **Bavarians** live in southern Germany. The earliest people to live in the area were Celts, who were subdued by the Romans before the Christian era. Later, tribes from Bohemia pushed along the Danube basin to settle in Bavaria. Frankish tribes were the next conquerors – by then the incursions of Slav peoples were halted. A benign climate and fertile homeland is reflected by the warm, jovial character of today's Bavarians.

The **Frisians** live in the coastal regions and islands of a stretch of Europe from the Zuider Zee in Holland, in the south to Jutland in the north. Their language is a form of German close to English. Unlike their neighbors the Frisians did not migrate during the Folkwandering period which took the Saxons and others through their lands to England. Today the Frisians proudly assert this identity as separate from their Dutch, German and Danish neighbors.

The **Germans** have complex ethnic origins. The Celts originated in south-west Germany and spread to most parts of Europe. The Scandinavian peoples mingled with early Germanic tribes and began what became the great Folkwandering period which took Gothonic peoples and languages throughout Europe. Later movements of Angles, Saxons and Jutes took Germanic people to England and the Low Countries. Until a hundred years ago, Germany was a patchwork of disunited states of peoples who spoke varieties of German. Slavic settlements were ethnically absorbed. The unification of the Germans (now again divided primarily through Communist Russian intervention) led to an afflatus of German militarism, temporarily masking the comradeliness, breadth of vision and instinctive loyalty that Germans combine with efficiency and drive.

The **Prussians** live in an area which includes the whole of Germany north of Saxony, Hesse and Bavaria. Their language, now Germanic, was originally closer to the Baltic dialects of Lithuanians and Letts. In the 13th century the Teutonic knights annihilated most of the heathen Prussian population and the territory was resettled by German peasants and townspeople. In recent times, the Prussian 'Junker' aristocracy has been a powerful militarist influence.

The **Swiss** speak four languages – German, French, Italian and Romansch – but thousands of years ago they were even more culturally and linguistically disparate. The Swiss mountains and valleys encouraged the isolation of small communities. In the late Iron Age Celtic tribes, of which the most formidable were the Helvetii, moved south from Germany along the Alpine frontier of the expanding Roman Empire. By the 9th century Germanic tribes had penetrated most of northern Switzerland, and the Gothonic dialects ancestral to modern Schwyzerdütsch (German Swiss) had been implanted. In the south and east a form of Latin had taken root among the Romanized people, and

Finn   Dane   Swede   Norwegian

lingers today among the highland peasantry as Romansch. French influences and language spread around Lac Léman in the west. The Alpine terrain consolidates Swiss unity; their fundamental cosmopolitanism has established a tradition of tolerance and neutrality.

The **Tyrolese** live in the mountainous Austrian Tyrol. In pre-Roman times they were close to the Alpine Swiss. When the Rhaetians, a Celtic-speaking tribe, occupied both the Tyrol and southern Switzerland Roman rule gave way to the Ostrogoths, a Germanic speaking people. Whether as citizens of the German or Austro-Hungarian empires, or of Italy, the Tyrolese have retained their genial and rich identity.

The **Viennese** live in the Austrian capital. More than other Austrians they were affected by the expansion of the Austro-Hungarian Empire when non-Gothonic peoples, mainly Slavic and Magyar-speaking, poured into the urban centers, principally into Vienna. An old established Jewish community contributed to the cosmopolitan nature of this city. Until World War II Vienna was Europe's most polyglot city. Its people are still known for their quickness and artistic creativity.

SCANDINAVIA AND FINLAND

The Scandinavians – the Swedish, Norwegian and Danish peoples – are unlike any other group in Europe: they can be regarded to a large extent as a culturally and linguistically homogenous people. Since neolithic times there has been far greater movement away from the shores of Scandinavia than to them – an irregular drainage of Scandinavia's sons which has altered the history of many European nations. The ancients called Scandinavia the Womb of Nations. The migrations of Goths and Vandals, Cimbrians and Teutons and, of course, the Vikings give substance to the term. Scandinavians traveled and settled as far as north Africa in the south and the Black Sea in the east. Few other Europeans entered Scandinavia except as slaves, vassal-wives or traders. As early as the 2nd century AD the main groupings had been established – the Swedes, the Danes and the Norsemen. All spoke early forms of a dialect of the Gothonic tongue. The long-ships, later to carry Scandinavians as far as North America, were used on short coastal raids.

Finns and Estonians, on the northern and eastern shores of the Baltic Sea, have a distinct Finno-Ugrian language and common ancestors (who forsook their homeland in central Russia in the early Christian era). They mingled both with early Gothonic people of the Baltic coastlands and with culturally backward forest people inland. The medieval colonization of Finland by Swedish kings resulted in a Swedish minority; and the Russian domination of Estonia results in new Russian élite.

The **Danish**. King Alfred's translation of the *History of the World* (9th century) contains the first reference to 'Denmark'. This was after many Danish tribes, notably the Angles, Jutes and Danes had imposed their language (already distinct from other Scandinavian tongues) and culture on many parts of western Europe – in particular Britain and France. The Viking expansion, Danish as well as Norwegian-based, was already under way. In more recent times over 300,000 Danes have emigrated to the US – leaving a well ordered nation rich in history and production.

The **Finns** came from an area between the Oka and the Ural mountains in central Russia. Their language, Finno-Ugrian, like that of the Magyars of Hungary, is not one of the Indo-European family of languages. Their nearest ethnic neighbors are the Estonians. Finns evidently began to arrive during the first few centuries of the Christian era, mingling with the native forest people and others – perhaps of Scandinavian origin – on the Baltic coastlands. More recent history has seen the Finns overwhelmed in turn by both Swedes and Russians. The Carelians, whose territory was recently annexed from Finland by the USSR, speak an archaic Finnish dialect. The Finns, less dour than Scandinavians, are warm and hospitable, and combine discretion with valor – both qualities needed by a small independent nation until recently colonized by so vast a neighbor.

The **Norwegians**. From ancient, probably prehistoric, times the Norsemen have been famed for their seafaring exploits. As Vikings they established colonies in Ireland, Scotland, the Faroes, Iceland and North America. Laws and constitution of modern Norway are the legacy of early Norsemen, and in Norway the justice of their system is admirably demonstrated. Norwegians combine a dour hardihood with depth of imagination.

The **Swedes** – the Suiones – appear in the literature of Rome. In the 6th century Goths are recorded as inhabitants of Sweden, when each tribe had its own king. Early in the 9th century Swedish kings gained control of the Baltic regions of present-day Russia; a land that yielded furs and slaves. The Swedes ruthlessly exploited the Slav people. Three centuries on the side-lines of world events has brought today's Swedes comfort, prosperity and perhaps a certain *ennui*.

143

Osset Circassian Caucasian Jew Armenian

THE CAUCASUS

In contrast to the flat, open lands of European Russia where the people are relatively homogenous, the Caucasus mountains between the Black Sea and the Caspian contain an astonishing number of different languages and peoples. The many valleys of the Caucasus are cul-de-sacs in which vestiges of all people who have passed this way during the past 2,000 years have been isolated and preserved more or less intact.

Linguistically the oldest established peoples are the Georgians, the Lesghians, the Chechens and the Cherkess who all speak dialects of the locally ancient Caucasic group of languages. Political changes, however, have radically changed their patterns of distribution. Large numbers of Cherkess migrated south after the Russian conquest, and thousands of Chechen and Ingush speaking people were resettled in central Asia after 1945.

Caucasians can also be sub-divided by their physical characteristics. A Russian anthropologist claimed to have identified 16 well-defined physical types in the region. Caucasic speakers, exemplified by the Georgians, tend to be short, dark haired and dark eyed. Ossets tend to be taller and fairer, and Armenians short and stocky, with acquiline noses and long faces characteristic of the ancient Hittites and Assyrians (who also featured the west European Jews, the Ashkenazim). The Caucasus gives an extraordinary insight into the migrations of peoples across south-eastern Europe, for here many were halted, and many have remained.

The **Abkhaz** live in a region of Georgia in the north-west on the Black Sea, bounded on the east by the mountains of the Kabardin region. Sukhumi, where an orchestra of centenarians plays twice a year, is the chief town. Since the 16th century, the Abkhaz have been Muslim. They speak a 'Japhetic' language.

The **Armenians** live both sides of the Turkish/USSR border. After Turkish persecution early in the 20th century many are now scattered all over the world. They are tall dark people, often with hooked noses. Their language is Indo-European and much closer to modern west European languages than most of those spoken in the Caucasus. The Armenians are noted for their industry and enterprise.

The **Chechens** live in the rugged central mountains of the Caucasus, and share the region with the closely related **Ingush** in Georgia. In the last century they were among the fanatical supporters of the great Muslim rebel Shamil. They still live on a communal basis, hunt, herd, and are famous dagger-makers. In 1944 Stalin transported them en masse to Siberia for alleged complicity with the Nazis.

The **Circassians** also known as the Cherkess, live in the mountains and plains of the north Caucasus and speak *adigheb*, a branch of the Pre-Indo-European 'Japhetic' languages found in other parts of the Caucasus. Till recently they had a

feudal system and slaves. Stalin dispersed them in 1943 for alleged sympathy with the Nazis.

The **Daghestanis** are mostly Lesghian people. They live in Daghestan, a fiercely Muslim region of the Georgian Republic. There are at least 24 Lesghian languages including Avar – the language of a European people annihilated in the 9th century AD.

The **Georgian** (or Kartvelian) language – similar to Laz, Svan and Mingrelian – is the most commonly spoken of the Pre-Indo-European 'Japhetic' languages that predominate in the Caucasus. The Georgian republic, with its capital at Tbilisi (Tiflis), stretches from the Black Sea to the Caspian. Much of the land is mountainous (Mt Elbruz rises to over 18,000 ft.). For over 2,000 years Georgia was a kingdom until she became part of Russia in 1801.

The **Kalmuks** are Mongol descendants who have lived for over 300 years in the north-east region of the Caucasus in the USSR. Some are Buddhist. They speak a Mongol tongue and have distinctly Mongol looks – round faces, slit eyes, yellowish skin. In 1943 Stalin transported them en masse to Siberia for alleged complicity with the Nazis.

The **Khevsurs** live in scattered groups in the most remote mountain regions of Georgia around Mt Borlalo. Their Georgian dialect is incomprehensible to other Georgians. They obey the law of

vendetta and are famous fighters. They mix Islam with Jewish, Christian and heathen customs – and keep the Christian, Muslim and Jewish sabbaths.

The **Lesghians** are a collection of tribes who speak at least 24 different languages of the Pre-Indo-European 'Japhetic' group. They live in Daghestan in east Georgia, where they continue their traditional way of life – hunting and stock-breeding. Most are fanatical Muslims.

The **Mingrelians** live on the Black Sea coast in south-west Georgia. Their Pre-Indo-European language and culture have for many centuries been very like that of the Georgians, who fully assimilated them into their kingdom. Some live in north-east Turkey.

The **Ossets** are descended from the Alans, a once powerful Iranic-speaking tribe who lived on the steppes north of the Crimea. They were swept into their Caucasian mountain refuge by the Huns in the 5th century AD. In the 12th century they became Christian, but later turned to Islam. In 1802, the Russians finally conquered them. They live 10,000 feet up in the mountains where, still defiant towards encroachers, they build defensive stone towers overlooking mountain passes.

The **Svans** are an isolated mountain people who live largely by hunting in south-west Georgia. Once capable of raising an army of 200,000, they now number about 25,000.